BURTON F. PORTER

the head &
the heart

PHILOSOPHY IN LITERATURE

Humanity
Books

an imprint of Prometheus Books
59 John Glenn Drive, Amherst, New York 14228-2197

Published 2006 by Humanity Books, an imprint of Prometheus Books

Inquiries should be addressed to
Prometheus Books
59 John Glenn Drive
Amherst, New York 14228–2197
VOICE: 716–691–0133, ext. 207
FAX: 716–564–2711
WWW.PROMETHEUSBOOKS.COM

10 09 08 07 06   5 4 3 2 1

Library of Congress Cataloging-in-Publication Data

Porter, Burton Frederick.
    The head and the heart : philosophy in literature / Burton Porter.
        p. cm.
    Includes bibliographical references and index.
    ISBN 1–59102–411–0 (hardcover : alk. paper)
    1. Literature—Philosophy. 2. Literature, Modern—History and criticism.
I. Title.

PN49.P674 2006
809'.93384—dc22
                                                                2006002860

Printed in the United States on acid-free paper

To Barbara,

who knows children are precious,
and enables them to thrive

TABLE OF CONTENTS

INTRODUCTION
The Relation Between Philosophy and Art

*E*mpirical matters and methods hold little appeal for the artist inhabiting a world of feeling and awareness, mood and insight. The scientist, for his part, has little patience with a mode of understanding that lies beyond verification; he concentrates upon discoveries about the physical universe rather than private emotions. A fundamental difference in methodology and subject matter thus assigns art and science to separate realms, and the great gulf fixed between them separates individuals of opposite temperaments.

The artist views the scientist as superficial and narrow, uncritically pragmatic, and deficient in sensitivity toward the more profound subtleties of existence. "What has the testing of hypotheses to do with imaginative understanding?" the artist asks, just as the religious man cries, "What has Athens to do with Jerusalem?" And the scientist charges the artist with arbitrariness and irrelevance, an irresponsible indulgence of feeling at the expense of genuine and practical knowledge; in a world overflowing with urgent needs and concomitant obligations, the arts serve only a distracting function. Thus each invalidates the other's activities out of hand, and they operate from radically different perspectives concerning what constitutes a legitimate concern, purpose, material, and approach.

Historically, philosophers have been divided in their loyalties between these two basic spheres. Long before the scientific revolution, a scientific viewpoint existed, which various philosophers valued and found eminently compatible with their discipline. Thinkers as distant as Aristotle and Bacon, for example, esteemed the rigor and precision of scientific method, which yielded concrete knowledge of nature and man. Science concentrated upon the objective world divorced from subjective impressions that distorted truth, and provided a model of procedure and standards by which philosophic theories could be judged.

Some philosophers within this tradition not only endorsed science but distrusted art for its emotive power. Art persuaded us to accept beliefs by generating a sensuous response, by engaging our passions and muddling our minds. It seduced us into assent by exploiting the emotional aspect of ideas rather than promoting the cool consideration of intellectual matters in terms of logic. Whether its language was color, melody, or poetic image, whether sympathy and agreement was engendered by a cathedral, a line of verse, or a piano concerto, art moved men to truth through beauty. Such an appeal was too uncritical and ecstatic to be trusted. Surely understanding of reality came about through argumentation and the dispassionate examination of alternative theories, by reflection and comprehension, thinking deeply not feeling strongly, through light not heat. Truth could be beautiful, but the beautiful is not ipso facto true. Art blurred this distinction through the suasion of its sensible forms, and induced men to believe nonsense clothed in affective dress.

Furthermore, art generally deflected attention from economic and political concerns, and to that extent could be morally condemned as deficient in humanity. Instead of improving the conditions of existence by developing superior social systems, artists directed their energies toward achieving moments of heightened awareness and influenced others to neglect their obligations as well and seek the momentary joy. An orientation of this kind is not only frivolous but also selfish, since aesthetic satisfaction is achieved at the expense of human welfare. How could Mozart have taken no notice of the French Revolution happening around him?

The indictment is severe but also a left-handed compliment, because tribute is being paid to the power of art to capture man's spirit and allegiance, and philosophy has, from time to time, defended this power as salutary to human progress and understanding. A viable case has been made for art as its own excuse, but that argument aside, perhaps the artist's contribution to the quality of human life surpasses that of politics even in its broadest Greek sense. Art offers man an intensification, enhancement, and expansion of life, which is unique unto itself, and people who lend themselves to the magic of Mozart or Homer or da Vinci can experience that enrichment which the moralist strives to realize in some distant Utopia. Rather than neglecting humanity, art offers life transfigured, existence rendered vital and luminous, vivid and delightful. Through the artist's vision the world yields its inner resonance and flavor, and daily living is raised from the level of banality to a vibrant, exalted plane. Surely moralists cannot criticize this elevation of life which art provides, for it is integral to their own ultimate ideal for human beings.

Additionally, people gain new insight through art in sudden flashes of awareness, which seems to argue against art as an impediment to truth. Undoubtedly one should be chary of a mode of appeal that defies verification and enchants the critical faculties rather than stimulating them, but perhaps art transmits truths that are otherwise unutterable and inaccessible. Perhaps through sensuous forms we come to realizations that transcend laboratory findings or the careful reasonings of the logician. At times we have all felt the superiority of artistic insights, and it would be mere prejudice to regard empirical and intellectual knowledge as more trustworthy than sensible and imaginative understanding.

When philosophers are struck by the veridical character of art, it is the intimate relation between art and the very quiddity of life that impresses them. The arts seem so directly in touch with essential reality that they take on a self-authenticating force. Any glib dismissal in terms of inconsistency or equivocation seems churlish. Criticism may be easy, but it is also hollow and cheap in the face of the immediacy and vividness that art provides. The idiom of the arts appears so profoundly suited to conveying the inner quality of life, the "inscape" of human experience, that philosophic theories seem poor abstractions by comparison.

Viewed in these terms art is not anathema to philosophy but perhaps indispensable in the quest for genuine understanding. It transmits through intuitive means insights unavailable to the rational processes of philosophy, a medium at once more personal and more compelling than syllogisms. And art may be recognized as compatible with philosophy not only in its truth content but in the coherence of its structure as well, which parallels the organization of reasoned argument. When the composer arranges his formal elements of pitch and key, timbre and color, harmony, melody, and rhythm into an aesthetically pleasing musical composition, or when the poet employs certain symbols and metaphors, a meter, rhyme, and form of verse to work his spell, the result appears strangely similar to a proof in Aristotle's or Spinoza's ethics.

What's more, the constructions of art present a worldview, a vision of nature, that seems philosophic. When art is didactic, showing our place in the universe, an ultimate meaning and destiny, it resembles the philosopher's system of metaphysics. Both offer a microcosm of life, whether on canvas, stone, or the printed page, and each is committed to the creation of a model that truly diagrams reality. *Les Miserables* is no less an interpretation of the human condition than *Being and Nothingness.*

The philosopher, then, may come to recognize a family resemblance indicative of a blood relation between art and philosophy. Perhaps philosophy is itself a kind of art, and the thinker an imaginative artist who descends within his mind, and through a blend of knowledge and inspiration, experience and logic, creates an intellectual work of art expressive of the universe as he conceives it. However far we may be prepared to go, at least the artist and the philosopher are not necessarily antagonistic; their disputes are probably family quarrels, and usually a complementary relationship exists between them. Thus Plato can award the Muses a place in disciplining the character of the youth, Schopenhauer can find liberation from the unceasing desires of Will in aesthetic contemplation, and Whitehead can maintain that individuality and personal development may be deepened through habits of aesthetic apprehension.

Sometimes, too, the arts may offer a vivification of philosophic concepts and problems, a more affective treatment of issues that involve the viewer, listener, or reader immediately and powerfully. The ideas expressed may not be novel or unknown to philosophy, but they receive an aesthetic force largely lacking in the discursive form of a treatise with its careful train of reasoning. Parallel themes may then be transmuted through art to an intense and personal level as, for example, in the following extracts, both of which treat the problem of evil.

In his *Microcosmus* Lotze states,

Of all imaginable assertions the most indemonstrable is that the evil of the world is due to the validity of eternal truth; on the contrary, to any unprejudiced view of Nature it appears to depend upon the definite arrangement of reality, beside which other arrangements are also thinkable, also based upon the same eternal truth. If there were retained the separation . . . between necessary laws and the creative activity of God, in our view evil would undoubtedly belong not to that which must be, but to that which is freely created.

Contrast this adultness with Dostoevsky's passion expressed through Ivan Karamazov:

Listen! If all must suffer to pay for the eternal harmony, what have children to do with it, tell me, please? It's beyond all comprehension why they should suffer, and why they should pay for the harmony . . . I don't want harmony. From love for humanity I don't want it . . . too high a price is asked; . . . And so I hasten to give back my entrance ticket (to Heaven), and if I am an honest man I am bound to give it back as soon as possible. And that I am doing. It's not God that I don't accept, Alyosha. Only I most respectfully return him the ticket.

These selections exaggerate the difference but illustrate the point. When a problem is treated artistically it takes on an emotive force usually lacking in either the critical or speculative approaches of philosophy. Ideas may be either enlivened or deadened by the vehicle conveying them, and although a tightly organized argument may appeal to persons oriented toward the cerebral, an artistic form tends to affect a wider audience and with greater power. Doubtless Kant is a more rigorous thinker than Shakespeare, but comparatively few are moved to evaluate their existence because of him, and that is not an indictment of human nature but a tribute to the power of art.

The philosopher may turn to the arts, therefore, not only to discover unique insights, fresh answers to stale questions, but to find his intellectual theories transfigured by a gifted artist into song. Such an examination will simultaneously add dimension and immediacy to philosophy, and make the artist conscious of the inner philosophic content of his art—something often hidden beneath feeling or form. As long as the philosopher does not murder to dissect, or deceive himself that art is nothing more than its cognitive part, the examination can be equally enriching to both the thinker and the artist.

The following chapters are an attempt to investigate this particular aspect of the relation between philosophy and art, specifically with regard to the philosophic content of literature. Hopefully the reader will be made aware of some important philosophic issues inherent in outstanding literary works, and find these issues infused with life by the imaginative skill of the literary artist.

1

LIBERTARIAN AND DETERMINISTIC PERSPECTIVES
Melville's *Moby Dick*

*T*he lifting of my finger is a metaphysical act. On the *libertarian* view it is an activation of atoms by an urge, a penetration of my will into space, and thus an emblem of my being. My thrust is of no physical significance to the infinitude of matter, but as a symbol of my presence, as a focusing of energy and a shift of substance in response to a whim, its repercussions are immense. This minimal act shakes the cosmos because it is internally chosen and unnecessary. Some spiritual center has initiated an event that moved into the realm of observable things, not as an effect of irresistible forces, but as the result of a playful impulse. And this center itself was not produced by prior factors that determined its character and decisions, but emerged concomitant with myself as an autonomous entity.

My identity is constituted by the free acts it engenders. With the power of will I am a demigod deliberating, deciding, and acting, or whimsically etching upon the extrinsic world with my fingernail, tickling fate under its chin. My thoughts have metamorphosed into physical form, transposed to a different order. I am creating or destroying with a divine arbitrariness and irrelevance, making a portion of the universe over to suit my predilections. My intentions are impressed upon the time-space manifold, changing its nature and demonstrating my significance.

My existence thereby matters. I can be arrogant toward inert objects, for law and necessity do not explain me. Free will, the postulate of gods and men, the condition for art and engineering, has placed me beyond the regularity that allows descriptive definition. Uniqueness and mastery are mine, signified by raising a finger. Reassurance of my sovereignty can be had at any time.

On the *determinist* view my act contains metaphysical import as well, for it becomes immediately linked to the casual chain extending forward and backward to vanishing points in time, an event in the universe of events, involuntary and predetermined. My finger has lifted in the same way as a stone drops: in accordance with natural law. No interior volition moved it, no mind containing a faculty of will, no spark of spontaneity.

This implies I am not accountable for my behavior, for the determinants lie wholly outside myself. I cannot be criticized for immorality or praised for a gratuitous move. I can be viewed only in the perspective of evolutionary history, the latest stress in the rhythm of cause and effect. The causal contexts of physics, chemistry, and biology; the social environment; and my organism's psychology act like interlocking gears. Isolation of myself is artificial and insolent when the synchronization becomes apparent. My knife-edge instant of time rests within the temporal dimension, and needs the chronological sequence of moments for its realization. My pinpoint of space is hemmed in by lines and planes pressing from without. My act is held within this framework, the necessary consequences of the conjunction of these dimensions and their alembic modes. Whatever happens results from a set of conditions, a specifiable setting, whether the events are mental or physical. All occurrences can be explained in terms of a pattern, and consequently are predictable in theory; the near future will bring the quantification and exact measurements required for the predictions.

Nature's mechanism is uniform and all-embracing. Its universality must be acknowledged by any person regarding the processes without vanity and bias, anyone mature enough to relinquish the dogmatism of his uniqueness. It applies to particles of matter and the largest celestial object, microcosm and macrocosm, the centripetal and centrifugal, rendering everything a means or an end, instrument or material. And this polarity circumscribes my actions, making uncaused choice impossible.

My role therefore becomes a subordinate and insignificant one. I am damned by the limits, which are incompatible with self-determination, yet also blessed by being within a paternal embrace, part of an ordered unity standing against chance and chaos. I am participating in an eternal pageant and tradition. There is the profound security of belonging as an integral part of the whole, not as an anomaly and an outcast. The spontaneous entity is a freak outside of nature, but here at least there is normality and integration. I am at one with life.

It is tempting to say that here, too, I possess the unique advantage of freedom from the anxiety of freedom. If I am a puppet in my movements, then the faceless puppeteer has made the choices and I am not responsible for what I do. I remain utterly blameless, without guilt, regret, or remorse.

But there is a sense in which responsibility does not exist whether men are assumed to be free or determined. Free acts, occurring fortuitously and unpredictable on impulse, cannot be attributed to a self. No continuous personality can be isolated as the source, for such an identification would have to be in terms of characteristic actions. We can speak of harmful occurrences, but not wrong acts or individuals who are indictable. The world contains evil but is without evildoers. And as indicated above, if actions are the unavoidable outcome of predetermined personalities, praise and blame are equally drained of meaning, not because there are no individuals, but because people cannot be held responsible for what they are compelled to do.

But this is a philosophical quibble without force to laymen or artists who associate responsibility with free will, and innocence with necessity. And, in fact, there are philosophical arguments that justify this customary response.

Determinism and libertarianism, then, are the two poles regarding conduct. Aristotle, Kant, Hegel, Spinoza, Descartes, Hobbes, Hume, Locke, and James have brooded and written about it with insight but without definitive success. Theologians have involved themselves as well, in pondering the relationship between free will and providence, for example. There seems to be an unanswerable paradox faced by the theist: If men are genuinely free to choose between options, then God does not possess foreknowledge and cannot be thought omniscient; but if freedom is only an illusion, then according to general notions of morality God should not punish or reward men for their deeds. If God knows what we *will* do, then it is what we *must* do and there is not choice. Either God's knowledge or his goodness are questionable, his nature problematical.[1]

Novelists, poets, and dramatists have found in the puzzle a dramatic catalyst of exceptional force. They have written of the claustrophobic writhing of humans trapped by fate or circumstances, and the elemental frustration of impotence. They have depicted the dread of destiny, doomed rebellions and escapes, inexorable sufferings—doubly intense for being unavoidable and undeserved, spirits broken flailing against the bars, or alternately the peace of submissiveness, the comfort of a future as fixed as the past, and the natural, childlike satisfaction of having an authority that sets limits and exercises control.

Under the assumption of free will, the power of the hero has been celebrated. Writers have exploited the archetypal response that human beings carry to the myth of the noble and courageous individual in command of his own energies and the situations confronting him. People want to bend a seemingly inflexible fate to their purposes, which is a large part of the appeal of magic and gambling as well as a genre of literature. In his masterfulness, the hero is the bearer of personal dignity, and everyone identifies with symbols of elegance and strength. Identification is also possible with the anxiety that choice entails, and the indecisiveness, liability, and apprehension involved; even trivial movements spread ripples that end in mystery, and thus in action there is always the fear of unknown consequences.

Protectiveness and oppression then are the ambivalent emotions generated by a deterministic universe. The double edge of indeterminism is exultation and anxiety. It is this network of passions that literature has often utilized with intense evocative power. Most generally, the hero's exultation is stressed and the oppression of a fated role, but there are exceptions that, of course, reinforce the generalization.

It is the Greek dramatists who have presented most vibrantly the pathos of human life lived in subjection to the gods—gods who exist in the Greek consciousness as capricious, unjust, jealous, and bickering beings. Or more penetratingly, they have shown all events as illustrations of moira, a more encompassing and impersonal destiny to which both gods and men are subject. Even the power of Zeus is thought compromised by moira.

The choruses carry the burden for making apparent the cosmic determinism that engineers the dramas. Euripides at the conclusion of *Medea* has his chorus declare, "Many a fate doth Zeus disperse, high on his Olympian throne; oft do the gods bring things to pass beyond man's expectation; that, which we thought would be, is not fulfilled, while for the unlooked-for god finds out a way; and such hath been the issue of this matter." Almost identical summations appear at the end of *Alcestis*, *Helen*, *Andromache*, and the *Bacchantes*. Sophocles uses his chorus to the same effect: "Alas, the dark dealings of the gods! Alas, hapless races of men, whose destiny exceeds due measure!" (*Philoctetus*). And near the end of *Oedipus Rex* the chorus, referring to Oedipus, chants, "O dread fate for men to see, O most dreadful of all that have met mine eyes! Unhappy one, what madness hath come on thee? Who is the unearthly foe that, with a bound of more than mortal range, hath made thine ill-starred life his prey?"

What a different temper exists in the tone and attitude of Edmund in *King Lear*:

> This is the excellent foppery of the world, that when we are sick in fortune—often the surfeit of our own behaviour—we make guilty of our disasters the sun, the moon, and the stars, as if we were villains by necessity, fools by heavenly compulsion, knaves, thieves, and treachers by spherical predominance, drunkards, liars, and adulterers, by an enforced obedience of planetary influence, and all that we are evil in, by a divine thrusting on. An admirable evasion of whoremaster man, to lay his goatish disposition to the charge of a star!

In other major works such as Tolstoy's *War and Peace*, Dante's *Divine Comedy*, Hugo's *Les Miserables*, and Goethe's *Faust*, various types of mitigated determinism appear under form of history's torrent, the will of heaven, the nexus of social conditions, or the limits of human possibilities, respectively. Some grid, some latitude and longitude constrain the characters' aspirations, thereby providing the framework for the art. Passion is held under the control of artistic form, which in turn derives from a metaphysical response to the human condition.

Moby Dick was created by Herman Melville using the tension of these wires, and its status in literature encourages investigation to some depth. Superficially a sea story peppered with adventure, the novel quickly expands to allegorical dimensions, and the reader is presented with a drifting world of good and evil, supernatural forces abstract and personified, primeval confrontations with nature and unclean spirits, all within a majestic parable.

The lyricism is compelling. We can find empathy with the irrationality from the outset because we are born along by a rhetoric that appeals immediately to the inarticulate yearnings festering in all of us. The rationale behind senseless hungers, the coherence of impossible desires is understood through our own experience of longing and loss, and a dim memory of outrage and defiance. We read of ritualistic contracts with a sense of familiarity, and find liberation in monologues that make our elusive frustrations more concrete, recognizable, and capable of recall. The myth spread before us is not a fiction but a reversion to elemental confrontations embedded in our being, a primeval fantasy with symbols that stir us beneath the rational level. One cannot ask more of a myth than it be prototypical and explanatory, uniquely relevant to private experience and common to everyone's interior world.

Interpretations of this megalith are manifold. Is the book really a dramatization of a compulsively insurgent Id in mortal conflict with the oppressive Superego of society—an Id which overpowers the Ego's normal regulating functions? Is it the perpetual strife of opposites: spirit against flesh, eternity against time, will against nature, or internecine warfare of madness against madness, the irrational against the irrational? Is it a vision of man's impulse to unite with the eternal in nature, with the infinite and supernatural, or a protest against the "heartless voids and immensities of the universe"? Is Ahab evil incarnate, or should he be thought a religious hero for committing himself with a total passion to absolute truth, however mistakenly apprehended? Is the white whale the demonic energies of the universe that extinguish the soul of man, or the mysterious divine spirit, "the very veil of the Christian's deity"? Is he fate or immortality, or the Presbyterian conscience, or the silent, inscrutable future, or the last phallic being of the white man?

We will not delve too deeply into the secret motto and hidden motive at work. Sober literary criticism per se is extraneous to our purpose. But interpretation is relevant insofar as it is instrumental and philosophically revelatory. Our main concern rests with the free will/determinism puzzle and how the drama vivifies it. To the sensitive ear it is apparent that a rhapsodic set of variations has been composed on the theme of fate.

The quest for the white whale is managed in every essential from offstage, and Captain Ahab, Starbuck, Pip, Queequeg, in fact every member of the crew including the narrator, Ishmael, play appointed parts in an archaic, recurrent epic. It is clear that a biblical myth is being reenacted against a majestic backdrop of sea, on a ship's deck instead of a desert floor, but still on a spacious canvas. Salt water has replaced sand as a caustic and scouring material, but the story's theme remains identical having been eternally ordained as a cyclical pattern of revolt and retribution.

Melville is truly a "transcendentalist in oilskin" who has both selected and created within the universal. He has described events and conditions that are manipulated by an irresistible hand. Every natural power is made a contrivance for enforcing a lawful arrangement upon the word; every disastrous happening on the *Pequod*'s journey becomes the implementation of a supreme will and a contribution to the ordering of man's unruliness.

In echo and shadow, Melville performs before us the biblical story of King Ahab, a man who provoked the God of Israel to anger by introducing the worship of baals, literally possessors of the soil, nature gods who held divine jurisdiction over stretches of fertile land. When the Hebrews were inhabiting Canaan, baal worship gained such force that shrines to local deities were erected on elevated ground within each province, and phallic symbols appeared in the form of stone pillars outside every shrine as indications of the fertile power of the god. It was this baalization of Yahweh that incited the rage of Hosea, and Elisha and Elijah, and provoked their prophecies of ruination. It was a profane change from unity to plurality, monotheism to polytheism, and from the high god of Moses to local spirits of nature.[2] The purer belief in Yahweh, transcendent and incorporeal, was being desecrated by worship of a materialized god tied to the seasonal sterility and fertility of the land. By promoting the baal cult, King Ahab broke Yahweh's first commandment, "Thou shalt have no other gods before me," thus rejecting God's dominion. It was not surprising that a stern, just, and jealous Lord exacted retribution; in a war against Damascus Ahab was mortally wounded, and willful defiance was rightfully punished.

No Jezebel appears in *Moby Dick* to influence Captain Ahab toward sacrilege, there are no war alliances and no treacheries, no literal or figurative calf worship. But the primary plot is the same: that of a blasphemous leader who rebels against divine authority and the laws of righteousness as revealed in Scripture, following natural responses instead of supernatural laws, choosing human judgment over God's holy will.

It is significant that Melville carries over the figure Elijah from the first Book of Kings—significant because Elijah is a prophet possessing foreknowledge that is uncanny. It is one thing for prophets to comprehend the future because of an understanding of the regularity of nature; insight into the relevant natural law is sufficient in itself to afford predictions. But it is quite another matter to interpret dreams and palms and meteorites; to read omens in a sheep's liver, signs in the flight of birds, a disposition in the arrangement of the stars, and a code in bone heated over a sacrificial fire. For if the universe is determinable in this way, then it is predetermined in its unfolding, and future events are already written. In this context primitive diviners (and biblical prophets) are men with charisma, gifted in foreseeing the historical outcomes of things. Sometimes their vision of doom is conditional, an if/then type; more often it is presented as a description of the inevitable. Notoriously their visions are dismissed, their words unheeded, and the prophecy is fulfilled. If strict predestination is operative, then, of course, the forewarning can have no practical use, and any escape moves by the victims are seen in retrospect as the fated means for bringing about a fated end.

It is prophecy in the sense of perceiving and disclosing what is foreordained that appears at the beginning of *Moby Dick*, and reveals the mechanism driving the narrative. "What signed, is signed; and what's to be, will be," Elijah says to Ishmael; "It's all fixed and arranged a'ready, and some sailors or other must go with him, I suppose." The ending is hypothetical for Ishmael; he could avoid the doomed voyage by taking the prophet seriously. But for Ahab, "the whole act's immutably decreed" as in a bloc universe, and he is the gear that winds the crew; his "one cogged circle fits into all their various wheels, and they revolve."

Ahab must fail, and this necessity drapes the story in black and governs its tragic clockwork. But what is he attempting? What particular sin does he commit that evokes divine censure as though sacred precincts had been transgressed and violated?

Overtly his crime consists in the determined pursuit of the white whale. "I'll chase him round Good Hope . . . and round the Norway maelstrom, and round perdition's flames before I give him up," Ahab vows. And again, "I'll ten times girdle the unmeasured globe; yea and dive straight through it, but I'll slay him yet." The whale had severed Ahab's leg with a scythelike sweep of his lower jaw as Ahab stood on a whaleboat's prow striking for a vital center with a harpoon. Now Ahab demands revenge. Whatever the ship's owners intend, the purpose of the voyage is not profit in sperm oil, but retribution; nothing will satiate Ahab but hunting Moby Dick to his death.

But a program of this character is wicked, as Starbuck protests: "Vengeance on a dumb brute! . . . [T]hat simply smote thee from blindest instinct! Madness! To be enraged with a dumb thing, Captain Ahab, seems blasphemous." God surely cannot allow a desire so steeped in evil to succeed.

There have been incidents in history when animals and even trees were held to be morally responsible agents, and court trials of such offenders are on record, but they belong to a milieu of ignorance, the twilight in which primitives grope and blunder.[3]

Ahab's act has no such mitigation, welling up as it does from within a civilized man, educed by low passions that have been allowed to dominate his intellect and sense of fairness. He proceeds despite awareness that unreasoning creatures are never accountable for their reactions.

Even if a man and not a whale had dismembered Ahab, his pursuit would be judged sinful from a Christian perspective because it would have been motivated by hate not love. Embodying the outmoded Talmudic conception of justice, Ahab is lashing out in reaction against an injury. Retaliation becomes his code, an eye for an eye, as he seeks the white whale's life in return for the indelible damage to his own. Christ's forgiveness for all wrongs, including blind injustices, never stays Ahab's will to be avenged. There is no idea in his mind of mercy or compassion, returning good for evil. Christian impulses never temper his will, but rather his fury forges his resolve and impels him on to destructiveness. In fine, then, Ahab sins not so much in wanting revenge on an animal devoid of malice, but in wanting revenge altogether.

In Melville's rendering such heathenism is loathsome to God—as intolerable in his sight as King Ahab's worship of baals, which stigmatized Ahab as the man who "did more to provoke the Lord God of Israel to anger than all the kings of Israel that were before him." Perhaps Baal stands to Yahweh and Yahweh stands to Christ, that is as an earlier conception of God belonging to the childhood of the race, superseded by a purer revelation to humanity.

As if to complete his own indictment, Ahab involves and implicates the crew in his sacrilege, thereby drawing fellow human beings to their deaths and to hell beyond as accomplices. That they are sometimes apprehensive and sometimes eager for the chase as their conscience waxes and wanes and their nerve fails and quickens, hardly diminishes the evil; they remain acolytes attending and furthering an unholy mission. The pagan harpooners Queequeg, Tashtego, and Daggoo readily lend themselves to the pact, free from the worry of Christian principles. In a ceremony sinister with manifest satanic symbols, they pledge themselves to vengeance and destruction as instruments of their captain: "Cut your seizings and draw the poles, ye harpooners!" Ahab commands.

Silently obeying the order, the three harpooners now stood with the detached iron part of their harpoons, some three feet long, held, barbs up, before him.

"Stab me not with that keen steel! Cant them; cant them over! know ye not the goblet end? Turn up the socket! So, so; now, ye cup-bearers, advance. The irons! take them; hold them while I fill!" Forthwith, slowly going from one officer to the other, he brimmed the harpoon sockets with the fiery waters from the pewter.

"Now, three to three, ye stand. Commend the murderous chalices! Bestow them, ye who are now made parties to this indissoluble league . . . the deed is done! Yon ratifying sun now waits to sit upon it. Drink, ye harpooners! drink and swear, ye men that man the deathful whaleboat's bow—Death to Moby Dick! God hunt us all, if we do not hunt Moby Dick to his death!" The long, barbed steel goblets were lifted; and to cries and maledictions against the white whale, the spirits were simultaneously quaffed down with a hiss.

Earlier the crew had been given their measure of grog from Ahab's hands:

"Drink and pass!" he cried, handling the heavy charged flagon to the nearest seaman. "The crew alone now drink. Round with it, round! Short draughts—long swallows, men; 'tis hot as Satan's hoof. So, so; it goes round excellently. It spiralizes in ye; forks out at the serpent-snapping eye. Well done; almost drained. That way it went, this way it comes. Hand it me—here's a hollow!"

It is, of course, a black mass, a ritualistic dedication to evil with Ahab as the devil's celebrant. All the classical inversions of the sacrament are not carried out—the sign of the cross is not made backward, or traced on the ground with the left foot instead of in the air with the right hand—but a perversion of the Eucharist is apparent. The harpooners stand three to three in a mock trinity with their irons upside down to form "murderous chalices." Maledictions not benedictions solemnize the communion, and authorization is imparted by the sun, an object sacred to heathen alone. Black blood has not been substituted for wine, but the grog, an impurity from the start, is unnaturally fiery, hot as Satan's hoof; this transubstantiation is not the blood of Christ, prince of peace, but an incitement to hate. And Ahab is no priest making supplication to his Lord, entreating mercy and favor, but a black magician tapping infernal powers, attempting to *compel* events to his design. If he can twist the souls of the crew to the same bent as his own, then an essential ingredient will have been added to the formula and a necessary condition for success will have been fulfilled. A ceremony conducted with the coolness of reason would never induce agreement from the ship's company; what's more, this mode of appeal is not natural to Satan or to Ahab's temperament. The heat and darkness of passion are demanded, and Ahab builds his ritual from this direction. The captive congregation quickly succumbs and the ship becomes the devil's ark.

In this ceremony alone there is enough cynicism and swagger to tempt any god to dispatch his Fates and Furies in pursuit, and perhaps the disaster stalking the *Pequod* is the justice due for desecration of a sacrament. Certainly Ahab, like his namesake, attracts the thunderbolt, and following Elijah's prophecies on the dock, other ominous happenings preview and token the collision of elements. No one involved can complain that the final cataclysm did not have long foreshadowing. The crew may have feared Ahab more than they feared fate, but the portents were obvious even to the least prescient. Melville continuously paints his tableaux in terms of inevitable punishment by the hand of God.

"Now mark [Ahab's] boat there," Starbuck says, "where is that stove. In the stern sheets, man; where he is wont to stand—his standpoint is stove, man." Elsewhere he exclaims of Ahab: "Has he not . . . dashed his heavenly quadrant? And in these same perilous seas, gropes he not his way by mere dead-reckoning of the error-bound log." And when Starbuck succumbs to the spell of the chase he muses, "Will I, nill I, the ineffable thing has tied me to him; tows me with a cable I have no knife to cut."

At the end, confronting annihilation, exasperated and terrified at the sinfulness and immortal danger, Starbuck shouts to Ahab,

> In Jesus' name no more of this, that's worse than devil's madness. Two days chased; twice stove to splinters; thy very leg once more snatched from under thee; thy evil shadow gone—all good angels mobbing thee with warnings:—what more wouldst thou have?—Shall we keep chasing this murderous fish till he swamps the last man? Shall we be dragged by him to the bottom of the sea? Shall we be towed by him to the infernal world? Oh, oh,— Impiety and blasphemy to hunt him more!

Other omens follow in the hawk striking at the ship's red standard, and the sharks that whittle the oars of the whaleboat—sharks that are later tame toward Ishmael as he floats in their midst. Ahab, of course, is not dissuaded by any number of omens. Previously when Starbuck acquiesced to his will, Ahab is so satisfied at the furtherance of his scheme that he fails to hear Starbuck's "foreboding invocation . . . nor yet the low laugh from the hold; nor yet the presaging vibrations of the winds in the cordage; nor yet the hollow flap of the sails against the masts, as for a moment their hearts sank in." These signs interrupt but do not disrupt his purpose. When his senses are more widely attuned and his circumstances understood, he exclaims, "By heaven man, we are turned round and round in this world like yonder windlass, and Fate is the handspike."

In a discursive passage Melville speculates that perhaps the determination is internal rather than external: "Ah, ye admonitions and warnings! Why stay ye not when ye come? But rather are ye predictions than warnings, ye shadows! Yet not so much predictions from without, as verifications of the foregoing things within. For with little external to constrain us, the innermost necessities in our being, these still drive us on." But he contradicts the conjecture by his customary language. The ship "blindly plunged like fate into the lone Atlantic" at the start of the voyage. The crew are "mortals ready and ripe for their fate," and are so weird in themselves and so officered that they "seemed specially picked and packed by some infernal fatality." Tashtego keeping lookout in the cross trees cries out with sounds that are musically strange and unearthly, "his hand stretched out like a wand . . . so wildly and eagerly peering towards the horizon, you would have thought him some prophet or seer beholding the shadows of Fate, and by those wild cries announcing their coming." When Ahab is the first to sight Moby Dick, he shouts, "Fate reserved the doubloon for me. I only; none of ye could have raised the White Whale first." During the chase that follows, the doleful eulogy uttered of the hunters is that "the hand of fate had snatched all their souls."

Melville's most explicit statement about destiny, which occurs when Ishmael is weaving an additional mat lashing for his boat, carries us light-years away from internal determinism. The passage justifies quotation in full:

> I was the attendant or page of Queequeg, while busy at the mat. As I kept passing and repassing the filling or woof of marline between the long yarns of the warp, using my own

hand for the shuttle, and as Queequeg, standing sideways, ever and anon slid his heavy oaken sword between the threads, and idly looking off upon the water, carelessly and unthinkingly drove home every yarn: I say so strange a dreaminess did there then reign all over the ship and all over the sea, only broken by the intermitting dull sound of the sword, that it seemed as if this were the Loom of Time, and I myself were a shuttle mechanically weaving and weaving away at the Fates. There lay the fixed threads of the warp subject to but one single, ever returning, unchanging vibration, and that vibration merely enough to admit of the crosswise interblending of other threads with its own. This warp seemed necessity; and here, thought I, with my own hand I ply my own shuttle and weave my own destiny into these unalterable threads. Meantime, Queequeg's impulsive, indifferent sword, sometimes hitting the woof slantingly, or crookedly, or strongly, or weakly, as the case might be; and by this difference in the concluding blow producing a corresponding contrast in the final aspect of the completed fabric; this savage's sword, thought I, which thus finally shapes and fashions both warp and woof; this easy, indifferent sword must be chance—aye chance, free will, and necessity—nowise incompatible—all interweavingly working together. The straight warp of necessity, not to be swerved from its ultimate course—its every alternating vibration, indeed, only tending to that; free will still free to ply her shuttle between given threads; and chance, though restrained in its play within the right lines of necessity, and sideways in its motions directed by free will, though thus prescribed to by both, chance by turns rules either, and has the last featuring blow at events.

Fairness requires the inclusion of this reflection just as honesty compelled the Gospels to record Christ's last ambiguous cry, and it is, of course, of theoretical interest in itself; an entire metaphysical system with ethical and political ramifications could be drawn from these suggestions. But Melville has not necessarily declared himself here. In fact, the book contains far too many inconsistencies for any single passage to be awarded primacy and the status of ensign: either it is immaterial which sailors accompany Ahab as Elijah suggests, or fate has specially picked and packed that particular crew. Either innermost necessities drive men on, or fate comes to meet them at a prearranged rendezvous that lookouts can foresee. Either chance invests events with their features, or destiny permeates everyone's history—the theory which Stubb expresses in its stoical form when he remarks, "Come what will, one comfort's always left—that unfailing comfort is, it's all predestinated."

But Melville, after all, is not explicating a consistent philosophical theory. As an artist, he works in affective spectrums to which a range of deterministic shades contribute. That there are clashing colors within this range is not a valid criticism; in fact, the writing is enlivened by the free use of varying perspectives. In interpreting any work, no single speech can be isolated as pivotal, but rather the entire range of words and actions must be regarded, the full context of Melville's art—an art which is unself-conscious and irrelevant as scholarship. After this is done quotations can be seen in their proper aspect, that is, as illustrations of positions central or peripheral to the overall theme, but never as proofs of it. Once we comprehend the general outline, these extracts become visible in their relationship to the whole and sense can then be made of them. Proof is always obtained silently through absorption. Quotations trumpet the news, which is why the proofs can never become illustrations, and illustrations are never proofs.[4]

If the novel is read in terms of divine determinism as suggested, then the eerie, arresting figure of Gabriel takes on fresh substance. Like Elijah, he assumes the posture in *Moby Dick* of an insanely accurate prophet, and like Elijah, too, he replays, somewhat in caricature, his former biblical role. In the book of Daniel he is depicted as explaining and announcing God's will, and according to Luke he stands before the deity, revealing God's purposes to men. Extra biblical literature portrays him presiding over powers himself, sometimes interceding for mankind, sometimes annihilating the wicked. The name "Gabriel" itself means "man of God," or "God has shown himself mighty."

In *Moby Dick* he appears in a rowboat maneuvering beside the *Pequod*, his craft tugged and cuffed by submarine powers, a bizarre figure even when measured against the extraordinary appearance of whaling crews. We learn that his shipmates on the *Jeroboam* revere him as charismatic, being so thoroughly under his spell that they defy their captain to fulfill his interpretation of God's will. Here is one prophet, at least, who rules above the king.

When Ahab declares his intention to hunt the white whale, Gabriel, who during his own ship's encounter with Moby Dick previously had screamed prophecies of speedy doom for attacking the whale, interprets the death of one of the mates. He cries out "with downward pointed finger—'Think, think of the blasphemer—dead, and down there!—beware of the blasphemer's end!'" And "down there" implies more than the sleep of death on the seabed, for a sinner's punishment is involved; Gabriel is promising eternal torment for Ahab's soul. It hardly takes a prophet to determine the fate entailed by sin, but Gabriel knows what constitutes sinfulness and how severely Ahab's sinfulness will be treated.[5] In this cognizance he has precognition and judges Ahab to be damned.

Gabriel exists as a fleeting revelation, the divine attitude made articulate in an unlikely form. He and Ahab rebound off one another, each gaining strength from the collision, and like mystic and materialist, hermit and philanthropist, saint and sinner, they are mutually dependent for differentiation. They find confirmation of their identities through each other, and a reinforcement of their selfhood in the increased self-examination that their conflict engenders. The prophet and the blasphemer are natural enemies, but they derive from each other the benefit of being locked more securely in their separate roles.

But why should Ahab be so dogged in his aims? He recognizes numerous warning signs, including that presented by Gabriel, yet he is not diverted. There is nothing to suggest he is a fool unaware of the risks or meager gains in success, yet surely it would be madness to persist in a venture blatantly marked for disaster simply for revenge against a beast.

The implication is that Ahab is stalking grander game. From the time when his leg was severed and he lay struggling for months in a hammock trussed around him like a winding sheet, until the moment he was resurrected on the *Pequod's* deck after remaining below "from Christmas to Quito spring," a moral metamorphosis was taking place within him. He emerged from his cabin not like Christ from the tomb, but as the product, agent, and victim of an opposite kind of transformation. Everything spiritual within him that formerly tended toward love, optimism, and peace had been replaced by righteous anger and manly rebelliousness. From an injured person he became a wronged one, for the cause was personified. He came to regard whales in general, and the white whale that had maimed him in particular, as intelligent, conscious beings, representatives of divine power, even God or the devil incarnate.

"Everything profound and terrible, all that is inscrutable and unjust is in the whale. Of all divers he has dived the deepest," Ahab ruminates in a dramatic monologue.

That head upon which the upper sun now gleams has moved amid this world's foundations. Where unrecorded names and navies rust, and untold hopes and anchors rot; where in her murderous hold this frigate earth is ballasted with bones of millions of the drowned; there, in that awful water-land, there was thy most familiar home. Thou hast been where bell or diver never went; hast slept by many a sailor's side, where sleepless mothers would give their lives to lay them down. . . . O head! thou hast seen enough to split the planets and make an infidel of Abraham, and not a syllable is thine!

When the whale is seen solemnly swimming, his head "overhung by a canopy of vapor, engendered by his incommunicable contemplations," it is "as if Heaven itself had put its seal upon his thought." And when one witnesses the "high and mighty godlike dignity inherent in the brow . . . that one broad firmament of a forehead, plaited with riddles; dumbly lowering with the doom of boats, and ships, and men," then one feels "the Deity and the dread powers more forcibly than in beholding any other object in living nature."

But the whale had done irreparable injury to Ahab, and if it is supernatural then the order of the universe is malevolent. The specific evildoer is the white whale that "dismasted" him, so that like a ship without sails he can hardly move, and this whale becomes the concentrated embodiment of the divine and cruel. In hunting him and pursuing vengeance, Ahab is not merely rejecting the Sermon on the Mount, but is also attacking the manifest Godhead. The power that was wielded had a spiteful character and engaged Ahab's rage. It energized his defiance as a humiliated being forced to endure existence in a condition that is a mockery of dignity and stature. Ahab perceives in Moby Dick "outrageous strength, with an inscrutable malice sinewing it." What could be a greater indignity to a proud man than a freakish, evil occurrence introduced without justice or explanation? "That inscrutable thing is chiefly what I hate," says Ahab, defining the nemesis, "and be the white whale agent, or be the white whale principal, I will wreak that hate upon him."

Ahab's aforementioned sinfulness in wanting revenge, and God's response, are now visible in deeper perspective. In pursuing the elusive and ferocious white whale, palpable but eternally elusive, it is the godhead that is being challenged. Ahab is both anti-Christ and anti–the Father. Without apology, he is opposed to the principles of the one person of the Trinity and the practice of the other. "Talk not to me of blasphemy, man!" he answers Starbuck. "I'd strike the sun if it insulted me."

Noli me tangere; nemo me impune lacessit (No one touches me; I am not struck with impunity) is his motto. The acts of the heavens that he observes and suffers do not inspire the love which is preached as precept, but, by example, fury and violence, even retribution as the ending demonstrated when God exacts his revenge. Such an exhibit warrants rebellion, and if an identical mentality is operative in the rebellion as that which provoked it, no excuse is necessary. If the universe truly had the character of a lamb, Ahab would worship its mildness, hold it precious and sacred, but saturated as it is with cruelty, a harsh response is demanded. In such circumstances ferocity is the only spirited possibility; a roar alone offers satisfaction.

When the masts of the ship are alight with St. Elmo's fire, looking like spermaceti candles congealed from oil in the hold, and Ahab feels the flame to be God's flame, God's force revealed and accessible, he chants his rebellion, creed, and apologia.

"Oh! thou clear spirit of clear fire," he addresses the Lord.

. . . I now know that thy right worship is defiance. To neither love nor reverence wilt thou be kind; and e'en for hate thou canst but kill; and all are killed. No fearless fool now fronts thee. I own thy speechless, placeless power; but to the last gasp of my earthquake life will dispute its unconditional, unintegral mastery in me. In the midst of the personified impersonal, a personality stands here. Though but a point at best; whencesoe'er I came; wheresoe'er I go; yet while I earthly live, the queenly personality lives in me, and feels her royal rights. But war is pain, and hate is woe. Come in thy lowest form of love, and I will kneel and kiss thee; but at thy highest, come as mere supernal power; and though thou launchest navies of full-freighted worlds, there's that in here that still remains indifferent. Oh, thou clear spirit, of thy fire thou madest me, and like a true child of fire, I breathe it back to thee.

Embittered by his crippled state, cheated of the possibility of full-bodied existence, Ahab walks the decks obsessed by the thought of divine malice. Unlike Job he cannot adore his tormentor, trusting in the goodness of the ultimate design. This is no long-suffering, faithful servant perceiving evidence of love in every disaster, assuming that who God loveth he chastenth. In Ahab there is neither boundless charity nor a masochistic temperament that condones pain, but a realism that takes events to be what they seem, and an animalism that reacts with brute simplicity to provocation. He lacks the philosopher's equanimity and that odd ability to turn experience upside down, to convert suffering to fulfillment, necessity to a virtue, all the negatives to a composite positive blessing. His blunt reflexes are antipathetic to rational deliberation. An animal is wounded, a human soul betrayed; the fury of animal and man join together singularly undeterred by the offender's might and magnitude.

Now the full pattern of Ahab's fatality is apparent from origin to deadly conclusion. God, as merciless power manifest especially in the whale, is the focus of Ahab's hate as well as the agent responsible for his necessary defeat when hate erupts as a challenge. Ahab is the tragic hero hopelessly throwing himself against an unconquerable force, sustained principally by a noble will. His mind is often aghast at the forces he faces, but he does not lose his nerve, and his conscience is as clean as a crusader's because a just cause is being championed. He feels he has been singled out for punishment and, at the same time, that he typifies all the pointless suffering of humankind. Fired by this belief, Ahab commits himself to redressing the moral imbalance by a simple rash lunge at the white incarnation of deity. An absurd scheme admittedly, yet more coherent than the universe, more finely ordered than a world ballasted with the bones of millions of the drowned, where unrecorded names and navies rust, and untold hopes and anchors rot. Unlike this morally senseless carnage, Ahab's enterprise possesses consistency and can be justified. It is only absurd in a practical sense, in terms of prudence and pragmatism, the tactician's aims. Ethically, in the light of Ahab's vision, the pursuit of Moby Dick is eminently sound and admirable.

God for his part cannot suffer such presumptuousness and spleen in a speck of matter gifted with the power of reflection. He is prepared for rejection as a possible consequence of endowing man with free will, and he will deal with the delinquents in due course, but a direct attack is unendurable. Such pride must be destroyed, and this necessity shadows Ahab's every move. At the end, God as whale, the whale with godlike force, attacks the ship, "vibrating his predestinating head," and destroys it utterly. "Retribution, swift vengeance, eternal malice were in his whole aspect," Melville reveals, "and in spite of all that mortal man could do, the solid white buttress of his forehead smote the ship's starboard bow, till men and timbers reeled."

In this ending God's physical superiority is evidenced, but his maliciousness is corroborated as well. He is the Old Testament God hating not only the sin but also the sinner, conceiving justice not in terms of needs but of deserts, a watchful and defensive being with strict limits of tolerance and a severe code of law. This God's sense of pride has introduced the possibility of offense (an impossibility to a selfless, wholly loving being), and retribution for offenses has become a natural concomitant. His biography (or autobiography) is filled with bloody acts committed in the name of a holy will and righteousness. He has condemned and destroyed Sodom and Gomorrah, devastated Ramses II's Egypt, and even drove his chosen people from their promised land when they departed from the Covenant. At one point he wiped out the entire sinful world except for the faithful Noah. In his jealously he visits the iniquity of the fathers upon the children unto the third and fourth generation of such as hate him, showing mercy only to them that worship him, and he promises that coals of fire, brimstone, and burning wind will engulf the wicked while the upright will behold his face.

To a being of such character, who awards love and salvation solely to those who keep his commandments, to a being who is beneficent but lacking in benevolence, the lawbreaker is an abomination deserving judgment without pity. Such a God could even punish those who serve him, as in the case of Job, for if he were required to reward the faithful, that would be a mechanical system, rendering God irrelevant. Acting out his nature and principles, God takes vengeance on Ahab. Thus in the cause for Ahab's death we understand the protest motivating Ahab's life. In the fact of his murder we see the justification for his struggle. In the manner of his end there is final vindication of his existence.

Had Ahab been forgiven as Christ forgave his persecutors, had he been spared or transfigured, then his battle would be ambiguous. We could question his vision of God as pure malice; the evidence would be mixed. We might be led to think that he was misguided all along, that his will had preceded his judgment, and his life purpose founded on a mistake. But in Ahab's destruction we perceive the correctness of his presumption that the universal order is malign. Human beings stand condemned, sometimes justly, sometimes not, and reprieves are a matter of whim; Calvin is much closer to the mark than Augustine. We can hold no expectation of clemency from an all-forgiving deity. Despite dogmatic assurances from apologists, the instances of suffering are far too numerous, obvious, and vivid to be explained away as myopia. Ahab has penetrated the obfuscations of theology, and confronts the natural world as a chamber of horrors.

The criticism could be pressed that Ahab's tragic mistake consists in fighting fire with fire, contesting evil with strength instead of love, and thereby becoming the very image of that which he hates.[6] But he has no other model before him, and although he might have imagined a world of opposite character, the imaginary could never move him like the immediate and real. In Ahab's experience the God who governs earth and water sermonizes in tempests and uproarious seas, earthquakes, floods, disease, and every variety of painful death. He is the creator of tigers as Blake points out, of sharks, as Queequeg remarks, the plague on the *Jeroboam*, and rapacious sea hawks with their own "fearful symmetry." The whale's serenity and quietude are "but the vesture of tornadoes."

To be godlike in Ahab's view means to be cruelly powerful and maliciously intelligent. The gospels speak of human brotherhood, compassion, and the gentleness of lambs, but the physical world exemplifies savagery so extreme that man with all his depravity has difficulty emulating it in degree and scope. It requires supernatural power to institute such terror. Ahab knows this personally as a direct casualty of natural evil, as the crippled victim of God's choleric force, but he is striking a blow for all humankind.

On any reading Ahab is a rebel against a hostile universe—and tragically rebellious because he confronts the omnipotent, but he is sometimes tantalizingly ambivalent about the identity of this enemy. Clearly it is the supernatural, but is it agent or principle, the incarnate or impersonal, God or the eternally inimical to man? Is Moby Dick "the gliding great demon of the seas of life," or "that intangible malignity that has been from the beginning"?

At times Ahab seems to be operating within the latter conception, and even to question whether there can be a god in a world so inconsistent with himself. Perhaps the heavens echo with emptiness, and what we take for deity is mere appearance, the illusion of the real. Eidos, quiddity, noumena may not reside within phenomena after all, only in layers without a core. Perhaps the pathetic fallacy is being committed universally and our personalities are being reified. Maybe we have projected our human qualities upon a soulless world, not so much a world of benign indifference as a vacuous one. We can hardly speak of natural events without ascribing intentions, because there is a profound need to render the external similar to our internal selves to create life in our own image. (It was a great day when biology discovered that ontogeny recapitulates phylogeny.) This propensity is reinforced in turn by customary linguistic usage that calls the wind fierce in winter and gentle in summer, the mountain forbidding, the shade merciful, the rain democratic—usage that articulates a deep-seated impulse to imbue every unconscious thing with a teleological character.

But if we strip aside our quaintness and provinciality inclining us toward a homocentric view, perhaps the universe would be found devoid of warmth and personality, rules and direction, utterly fatherless. Humans might be worse than orphaned, an accidental by-product of random energy, a pointless pulse beat in one of an infinite series of rhythmic cycles that are equally futile. Even if expansion and contraction is not the governing process but the universe is expanding indefinitely, it would be hard to judge life meaningful in any objective sense.

The textual evidence is that Ahab alternately considers himself inhabiting just this type of world in which bad faith supports our desires. However, he is not sure, and he cannot be certain until he attacks the divine essence to test whether it is substantial or delusive.[7]

In reply to Starbuck's charge of blasphemy, Ahab answers,

> Hark ye yet again,—the little lower layer. All visible objects, man, are but as pasteboard masks. But in each event—in the living act, the undoubted deed—there, some unknown but still reasoning thing puts forth the moulding of its features from behind the unreasoning mask. If man will strike, strike through the mask! How can the prisoner reach outside except by thrusting through the wall? To me, the white whale is that wall, shoved near to me. Sometimes I think there's naught beyond. But 'tis enough. He tasks me; he heaps me; I see in him outrageous strength, with an inscrutable malice sinewing it. That inscrutable thing is chiefly what I hate; and be the white whale agent, or be the white whale principal, I will wreak that hate upon him.

Symbolically or actually to Ahab, the whale is the opaqueness of events which may be devoid of ultimate logic, merely an incoherent series of evil happenings that impede the human struggle for peace. That the whale seems to be totally silent even during his destructive furies adds force to his image as the manifestation of inscrutable malice: "the fear of this vast dumb brute of the sea was chained up and enchanted in him; he had no voice." And elsewhere, "The great genius of the whale . . . is declared in his pyramidical silence."

Even more compelling is Moby Dick's extraordinary whiteness, for white is primal and ambiguous in implication. It suggest the purely spiritual, "the very veil of the Christian's Deity," but also the intensifying agent in things most appalling to mankind. Tellingly Melville writes, "by its indefiniteness *it shadows forth the heartless voids and immensities of the universe,* and thus stabs us from behind with the thought of annihilation . . ." (italics mine).

In a chapter wholly devoted to the whiteness of Moby Dick and its overall significance, Ishmael meditates that it is

not so much a color as the visible absence of color, and at the same time the concrete of all colors; is it for these reasons that there is such a dumb blankness full of meaning, in a wide landscape of snows—a colorless, all-color of atheism from which we shrink? . . . The great principle of light, forever remains white or colorless in itself, and if operating without medium on matter, would touch all objects, even tulips and roses, with its own blank tinge— pondering all this, the palsied universe lies before us a leper; and like wilful travellers in Lapland, who refuse to wear colored and coloring glasses upon their eyes, so the wretched infidel gazes himself blind at the monumental white shroud that wraps all the prospect around him. And of all these things the Albino whale was the symbol. Wonder ye then at the fiery hunt?

The opaque and irrational, the heartless voids and immensities of the universe foreshadowing annihilation, the blank white shroud of the atheistic perspective—at key speculative moments Ahab is portrayed probing the entire metaphysic contained and implied here.

But can a world without deity, a world consequently lacking the consciousness necessary for deliberate action be condemned in its functioning? Isn't Ahab confused in calling bad what is only unfortunate, and railing against an unknowing, guiltless sky? Can an impersonal universe be considered evil?

Ahab behaves as if the world can be judged, for without conscious intention it produces effects that cause people pain. In effect, natural conditions may surpass any diabolical scheme in sheer weight of suffering, and human history can consist of little but man's efforts to control the extent and degree of recurrent disaster. As it is we shelter in houses against the earth's climate, the cold, heat, and rain; predatory and poisonous creatures; catastrophes such as avalanches, floods, blizzards, and fires; the deserts, swamps, jungles, and wastelands—never acclimatized, never at ease, perpetually estranged from nature, awaiting the final blow of death.

Even apart from the pain accompanying our sensible existence, the universe is brutal in operating with an efficiency devoid of love. If we must, of necessity, populate an insignificant edge of the universe without support from a god or justice or life after death, that in itself is cause for complaint. If we must live two by two to endure our aloneness, our only comfort other people in the same state, cosufferers of limited help and goodwill, surely this is a refined and subtle form of pain. There is nothing of cosmic value that would make human effort meaningful.

We cannot love this type of setting. At best we can only stand in awe of its magnitude and respect the vastness of its power and dimension. We surely cannot feel that life is meaningful, but that being has become self-conscious in man only to realize the pointlessness of being. We are exposed to the natural operations of time, including an animal death, without a deity to intervene on our behalf or even transform the banality. On these terms human life is mocked and made vain. No loving father can be prayed to as promised in Christian childhood, only an oblivious on-rolling of matter and energy with no one to blame for our condition.

To refine the point, just as Camus sees absurdity as not a characteristic of the unconscious universe but as residing in the disparity between our demand for meaning and the inco-herent succession of events, so we can see evil not as cosmic intention but as the disappointment of man's need for mean-ingfulness. In terms of the physical and psychological envi-ronment, nothingness can be even more painful to endure than persecution: we are without hope of grace.

But if there is nothing rather than something, if Ahab is at times attacking a purposeless void rather than a malevolent godhead, can we still regard the events as determined? A jealous god must crush rebellion, but surely what is oblivious to man cannot take affront and react to his provocations.

Here logical entailment ends and dramatic considera-tions reveal themselves. Without compulsion to do so, Melville utilizes a deterministic structure for the enhance-ment of his art.

It is not an unusual decision. Numerous writers have rec-ognized that an atmosphere of looming, inevitable catas-trophe affects an audience much more than surprise endings. The unexpected is an ingredient of comedy. Tragedy de-mands the strict unfolding of its inner laws. The oak inherent in the acorn, the person compressed in the chromosomes must be realized, and although we know the end, we are mes-merized by the means. Through morbid fascination, sado-masochism, or something more profound moving oceanically within us, we receive aesthetic enjoyment from the inevitability of a drama. And as Aristotle pointed out, the impact is heightened when a great man and a superior force conflict, resulting in the person's necessary downfall.

It is this gigantomachy that is portrayed in *Moby Dick*, together with all the affective advantages of inevitability. We are never in doubt that Ahab is fulfilling the terms of his destruction, but this certainty augments our interest rather than reduces it.

Whether the white whale is malevolent or indifferent, nature is red in fang and claw, and Ahab is destined for defeat. Melville is ambiguous about the whale, vacillating between the personal and impersonal malignity, but Ahab's necessary destruction is inherent in the plot. In the main, the identification of the whale as God prevails, and a divine determinism is operative as the drama's guiding principle. Ahab is fated for death as the divine response to his challenge. It is the deity's final answer to Ahab's relentless questioning—a cause and effect reminiscent of Oedipus. But unlike Oedipus, Ahab is not unknowing; his is a conscious engagement with omnipotence. The final chapter is foreknown as well as being foreordained. Given Ahab's determination to destroy the white manifestation of deity, the occurrences are patterned in inevitable sequence.

The phenomenal events then are unavoidably decreed; escape is an impossibility. Nevertheless, in a significant sense Ahab is free. He does not have the freedom to defeat the whale but he possesses free will. For to possess free will is not necessarily to effect what one wills, but to be free to will it.

Being in prison takes away a great deal of freedom of choice, especially with regard to movement. If B. F. Skinner is right, we have no free will since all of our behavior is a response to given stimuli. The distinction is between freedom, which enables us to do what we want, and free will, which is the ability to decide what we want to do.

Internally Ahab rules himself; externally his efforts are pointless, for the outcome is already written in infallible scriptures. Logically, of course, he cannot overpower an omnipotent force, but he is free insofar as he resists the inevitable. In Ahab's case, his actions result from his character, not his character from his actions, and being inner-directed, his soul remains inviolate.

It lends confusion that Ahab is unsure of his own autonomy, as when he says (partially in self-justification), "I am Fates' lieutenant; I act under orders." And elsewhere he muses, "What is it, what nameless, inscrutable unearthly thing is it; what cozening, hidden lord and master, and cruel, remorseless emperor commands me; that against all natural lovings and longings, I so keep pushing, and crowding, and jamming myself on all the time; recklessly making me ready to do what in my own proper natural heart I durst not so much as dare? Is Ahab, Ahab? Is it I, God, or who, that lifts this arm?" But he has neither been charged with the spirit of God nor possessed by a demon, and an obsession cannot be equated to the compulsions of a monomaniac. If he were mad perhaps determinism would be present, for in a sense the insane person acts according to type; his behavior is predictable. What's more, Ahab's unreasonable persistence does not mean the absence of self-determination, for it's not only reasonable actions that are free. Ahab is forever himself; Ahab, the person, is Ahab the universal symbol. Unsubmissive, disobedient, unrepentant, he is not the servant of any powers evil or blessed.

After repeated warnings God does take Ahab's life, consigning him to the depths, but in this cancellation there is a bow, an act of homage. Not only is it momentous when individual sin provokes cosmic punishment, but in the act of negating Ahab's rebellion, tribute is paid to his freedom and strength. Nothing that occurs can be utterly nullified and Ahab's protest remains, a created image of resistance to a brute world.

We have a parallel image in Prometheus who defied the godhead despite the hopelessness of such rebellion. In the account by Aeschylus he stood against Zeus, who intended to destroy humankind, opposing potency with cleverness. He is considered humanity's benefactor, bringing not only knowledge of the sciences and the arts, but also fire, the means for maintaining life. According to the legend, Prometheus smuggled it out of heaven hidden in a hollow stalk of fennel. For thwarting the divine will Zeus chained him to a mountain rock in the Caucasus, where he endured the unending punishment of having his liver consumed by an eagle daily and restored nightly.

Like Ahab, Prometheus's position is a doomed one from its conception, entirely damned in concept. He cannot hope to elude the wrath of Zeus even though he is an arch trickster. Through his gift of foreknowledge he knew that diurnal pain awaited him as a consequence. Self-concern surely dictated submission to the authority of Zeus, the most powerful immortal, perpetually armed with thunder and lightning. Nevertheless, Prometheus ignored the prudential alternative and elected to suffer for the good of humankind. In addition to his foresight he possessed vision. Premeditatedly he chooses a stratagem of resistance to Zeus's intentions, a course of sacrifice for humanity with full awareness of the retribution that will follow. It is a free choice of martyrdom and a supremely moral stand against an oppressive divinity.

A similar spirit is evinced by Satan in *Paradise Lost*, although his rebellion against the godhead is not for the sake of humanity or any mode of altruism. As a cruel means of gaining revenge and expanding the borders of Hell, he attempted to usurp God's power and bring about man's fall. It is not through love that Satan acted but through perverse desires. Above all else he wanted vengeance. He opposed Christian repentance with a gospel of sweet revenge, Christ's meekness with warfare, brotherhood with animosity. His goal was self-aggrandizement, his values splendor and magnificence, his means a plot for fomenting chaos by mingling hell and earth. If creation cannot be destroyed to nothingness at least harmony can be reduced and extended toward anarchy. With all the elements disordered, and confusion between truth and falsehood, reality, and illusion, Satan would necessarily rule as prince of deception. The pain that God would then feel at the state of creation, at man's involvement with sin and rejection of goodness, would gratify Satan in his hatred. Misery would dominate the universe, and God will have been repaid for casting the archangel out of heaven.

Of course Satan cannot assault creation without harming himself; destruction when it is absolute includes self-destruction as well, which is a wisdom Satan shares with nuclear-age citizens. But he is so intent upon revenge that he will knowingly increase his misery to the omega point simply to gain his ends.

None of this appears commendable except Satan's spirit, his dauntless courage in the face of transcendental denial, ostracism, and the utter impossibility of reconciliation with God. Regardless of his deviousness, ultimately he must be defeated in attempting to undermine God's might. The Lord is supreme, not only in power and wisdom, but in the higher virtues of justice and forgiveness, which qualify his attributes, and which Satan is constitutionally unable to emulate. His cause, therefore, is a lost one. Nevertheless, he continues to battle against "Heav'n's matchless King," and there is something enviable in an irrepressible spirit just as something gross resides in the Stoic's reasonable restraint when passion is futile. Mammon's attitude is strangely wholesome when he debates, "Suppose (God) should relent and publish Grace to all, on promise made of new Subjection; with what eyes could we stand in his presence humble, and receive strict Laws impos'd . . . how wearisome Eternity so spent in worship paid." And is it only through fancifulness or romanticism or because we are fallen creatures that our response to Satan quickens when he declares, "Better to reign in hell than serve in heav'n"?

We probably respond to Prometheus and Satan, Peer Gynt, Faust, and Caligula as if they were spokespersons for our resentment, vicariously relishing their resilience and rage, their voicing of our defiance as the cosmically oppressed. Somehow figures of this unusual depth and will, embodying an extraordinary spirit, are exempt from customary ethical evaluation. The rules governing commonplace behavior are simply inapplicable to the extremes of heroism. To try to judge their conduct in terms of universalizability, reasonableness, or social cohesion is beside the point. We can only stand back, removed from contact by their amorality, reduced to a state of admiration.

Surely this is the case with Ahab. He and the whale are involved in an unearthly confrontation that provokes a response of attraction-repulsion.

To the very end Ahab's spirit remains unbroken. Even after his boat is splintered by the white whale, in those moments which should have been filled with shock and despair, Melville writes:

> Dragged into Stubb's boat with blood-shot, blinded eyes, the white brine caking in his wrinkles; the long tension of Ahab's bodily strength did crack, and helplessly he yielded to his body's doom for a time, lying all crushed in the

bottom of Stubb's boat, like one trodden under foot of herds of elephants. Far inland, nameless wails came from him, as desolate sounds from our ravines.

But he inquires whether the men (and the harpoon) are safe, and, regaining himself, tries to stand. "Hands off from me!" he tells Stubb, who tries to help. "The eternal sap runs up in Ahab's bones again!" He yields to his *body's* exhaustion for a time, and in the final combat with Moby Dick, succumbs to his inherent mortality, but in his "proper and inaccessible being" he is whole. "Even with a broken bone, old Ahab is untouched," Melville writes. And Ahab says of himself, "ere I break, ye'll hear me crack; and till ye hear *that*, know that Ahab's hawser tows his purpose yet."

NOTES

1. There is a philosophical question concerning whether foreknowledge implies foreordination, which Chaucer in *Canterbury Tales* puts as follows:

That in the schools there's a great altercation. In this regard and much high disputation. . . . Whether the fact of God's great foreknowing makes it right needful that I do a thing (By needful, I mean, of necessity); Or else, if a free choice he granted me, to do that same thing, or to do it not, though God foreknew before the thing was wrought; Or if His knowing constrains never at all, save by necessity conditional. ("The Nun's Priest's Tale")

In book 4 of *Troilus and Cressida* (140–154), Chaucer provides an answer.

2. To make the godhead more accessible, people have often turned to a more physical conception of him. However, if the

divine being becomes too human, as in late Greek and Roman polytheism, he loses distance and dignity and is no longer respected or worthy of worship. If on the other hand the godhead becomes too spiritualized, then he is remote and impersonal, thereby failing to satisfy the emotional need for communion. This is one of the dilemmas of religion that Christian theology mitigates through the person of Christ, spirit incarnate.

3. It has been reported that in Lavergny, France, in the Middle Ages a sow and her piglets were put on trial for eating a man. The court found all of them guilty and ordered capital punishment for the sow. The piglets' sentence was commuted on the grounds of their youth and the bad example of their mother!

4. The same might be maintained with regard to intellectual arguments, that is, that credence is purchased not by the weight of debate points (for an argument can be valid but unconvincing), but through something infinitely more subtle, a sudden awareness and assent, a blaze of comprehension transcending the quantity or quality of factors presented. Various points can then be employed to illustrate the position that has been accepted, even the same ones which previously proved ineffective, but they have actually become superfluous and serve as rationalizations and not demonstrations. I believe Gestalt psychology can best explain the mechanics involved. But the reader cannot be convinced of this position, although perhaps he will agree with it and find the analysis subsequently meaningful.

5. All prophecy, of course, cannot be reduced to an understanding of theodicy, for this would imply unalterable rules of behavior for God. In Christian theology at least the mechanical analogy is rejected and free will is attributed to God. He is thought capable of acting in unusual ways. Hence the true prophet possesses not only knowledge of God's laws and nature, but foreknowledge of events as well.

In this connection one puzzle that has provoked theological debate is whether God can do what is contrary to his character (especially his goodness). If not, his omnipotence is threatened. If so, his absolute love becomes problematic.

6. In *Herman Melville* Lewis Mumford (New York: Literary Guild of America, 1929) writes,

[Ahab] has lost his humanity in the very act of vindicating it. By physical defiance, by physical combat, Ahab cannot rout and capture Moby Dick: the odds are against him; and if his defiance is noble, his methods are ill chosen. Growth, cultivation, order, art—these are the proper means by which man displaces accident and subdues the vacant external powers in the universe: but to become more human. Here is a hard lesson to learn: it is easier to wage war than to conquer in oneself the tendency to be partial, vindictive, and unjust: it is easier to demolish one's enemy than to put oneself against him in an intellectual combat which will disclose one's weaknesses and provincialities. And that evil Ahab seeks to strike is the sum of one's enemies. He does not bow down to it and accept it: therein lies his heroicism and virtue: but he fights it with its own weapons and therein lies his madness. All the things that Ahab despises when he is about to attack the whale, the love and loyalty of Pi, the memory of his wife and child, the sextant of science, the inner sense of calm, which makes all external struggle futile, are the very things that would redeem him and make him victorious. (p. 186)

7. Ahab is not a man to settle for the comfortable answer; only the honest one will satisfy him—an attitude that Melville justifies in a reflective passage:

Glimpse do ye seem to see of that mortally intolerable truth that all deep, earnest thinking is but the intrepid effort of the soul to keep the open independence of her sea; while the wildest winds of heaven and earth conspire to cast her on the treacherous, slavish shore?

But as in landlessness alone resides the highest truth, shoreless, indefinite as God—so, better it is to perish in that howling infinite than be ingloriously dashed upon the lee, even if that were safety. For worm-like, then, oh who would craven crawl to land.

Perhaps Ishmael's humanism in the "squeeze of the hand" passage is a capitulation that Ahab refuses. "Would that I could keep squeezing that sperm forever!" Ishmael says. "For now, since by many prolonged, repeated experiences, I have perceived that in all cases man must lower, or at least shift, his conceit of attainable felicity; not placing it anywhere in the intellect or the fancy; but in the wife, the heart, the bed, the table, the saddle, the fireside, the country; now that I have perceived all this, I am ready to squeeze case eternally."

Ahab, too, has his moment of repentance for his hubris:

The lovely drama in that enchanted air did at last seem to dispel, for a moment, the cankerous thing in (Ahab's) soul. That glad, happy air, that winsome sky, did at last stroke and caress him; the stepmother world, so long cruel, forbidding, now threw affectionate arms around his stubborn neck, and did seem to joyously sob over him, as if every one, that however willful and erring, she could yet find it in her heart to save and to bless. From beneath his slouched hat, Ahab dropped a tear into the sea; nor did all the Pacific contain such wealth as that wee drop.

But this craven crawling to land is atypical.

THE GOOD AND THE RIGHT

Anouilh's *Antigone* and
Tolstoy's *Anna Karenina*

*T*he whole of ethics is contained within these two notions; they are sometimes mutually exclusive and together comprise the subject matter of moral philosophy. All other problems such as whether one should fulfill oneself or serve others, or whether values imply prescriptions are reducible to either or both concepts. Even the debate over whether the moral quality of an action is primarily determined by its consequences or the intention of the agent is a derivative concern. First we must decide what is good and what is right, with valid reasons justifying our decision, and having answered this basic question we can then turn to peripheral issues with an easy conscience.

"Right" refers to actions that are ethically correct—usually in terms of specific rules of conduct. A philosopher might, for example, defend the rightness of honoring commitments or turning the other cheek, and argue against treating people only as means. Praise or blame is then assigned according to the extent to which a person's behavior conforms to these principles. Sometimes conscience is invoked as the arbiter, or perhaps societal approval and disapproval, but whatever standard is taken as authoritative it is actions that are assessed as right or wrong.

"The good" in contradistinction to "the right" means that which is a worthwhile goal in life, the ethically desirable aim or end of existence to which people should aspire.[1] It is the ultimate reason for living (or dying, as Camus notices) and the sovereign purpose that motivates our basic life choices. Whatever people posit as being of fundamental and intrinsic importance, the pivotal value around which they range their lives constitutes their conception of the good.

That is not to say that whatever is desired is necessarily desirable, that is, worthy of being desired. Critical philosophy will insist upon sound reasons for definitions of the good. But whatever satisfies the requirements is taken to be the ideal for human beings to achieve.

THE GOOD

There has been no shortage of candidates for the title of good; philosophy has been oversubscribed for centuries. But the credentials of the contenders are in dispute, and this confusion as to what is sufficient justification for naming something good leaves the issue moot.

Aristotle declared happiness to be the "one ultimate End," ". . . that at which all things aim." To his mind there seemed almost unanimous agreement on this point, which lent weight to the contention (as if ethical questions could be decided by counting heads). People differ in what they take happiness to be, some thinking it is satisfaction of appetites, some honor, and others moneymaking. Disagreements occur over the definition of happiness, but there is broad consensus about happiness being the good; after all, happiness is something self-sufficient (we lack nothing when we are happy) and it is always chosen "for its own sake and never as a means to something else"; it is "the end of all things done by human action." On the basis of these considerations, Aristotle rests his case.[2]

The ancient Greek philosophers Aristippus and Epicurus endorsed a kindred theory, each in his own way. Both affirmed pleasure as the good interpreted by Aristippus the Cyrenaic as sensual pleasure, intense, immediate, and brief, and by Epicurus as the tranquil, durable, and passive pleasures of the mind. Epicurus had the depth and mentality to develop a strong theory, and he is the more philosophically interesting of the two.[3] In one of the fragments he writes, "I know not how I can conceive the good, if I withdraw the pleasures of taste, and withdraw the pleasures of love, and withdraw the pleasures of hearing, and withdraw the pleasurable emotions caused to sight by beautiful form." This is worth pondering even though it makes pleasure necessary but not sufficient to good; that is, it is only associated with it. But there is a common sensibility in his words and a celebration of living which is hard to resist. It is reminiscent of Homer's cry: "Dear to us ever is the banquet and the harp and the dance and changes of raiment and the warm bath and love and sleep."[4]

Jeremy Bentham and John Stuart Mill in the nineteenth century reaffirmed the primacy of pleasure or happiness (conflating the two) although, having a social conscience, they rejected individualistic hedonism in favor of a universalistic doctrine—a utilitarianism promoting the maximum pleasure for the maximum number of persons in the community. Bentham states categorically, "[P]leasure is in *itself* a good—nay even, setting aside immunity from pain, the only good; pain is in itself an evil—and, indeed without exception, the only evil." (His reference to immunity from pain harks back to the Epicureans, who valued avoiding pain above seeking pleasure—an attitude for which the walled garden of Epicurus is a fitting symbol; it walled trouble out rather than walling enjoyment in, rather like a medieval city.)[5] He refused to recognize differences in kind with regard to pleasure or happiness but only in amount, and constructed a calculus for the precise measurement of the pleasure quotient to be derived from any given action. In this way it could be scientifically determined which act yielded more pleasure for more people and consequently was more moral.

Mill endorsed universalistic hedonism in turn but found the notion that poetry is as good as pushpin repugnant. Qualitative distinctions between pleasures were necessary as refinements of the utilitarian doctrine and basic to the establishment of an ethic consistent with the dignity of human beings. It is the higher, human pleasures that constitute the good and should be maximized for humanity. "It is better to be a human being dissatisfied than a pig satisfied; better to be Socrates dissatisfied than a fool satisfied."

Unfortunately, this welcome corrective weakens rather than strengthens the notion of pleasure as good. For "better" and "worse" must refer to some standard outside hedonism which then replaces pleasure as the criterion for morality. And if being a dissatisfied person is better than being a satisfied animal, then being human is ethically superior to satisfaction or pleasure.

From time to time in intellectual history, self-realization theories have appeared, often in unexpected quarters geographically separated from similar expressions of the same position. England and the United States appear to have provided the most fertile breeding ground, and the nineteenth century the best climate, for the ethic thrived as nowhere else and never before: F. H. Bradley, T. H. Green, Josiah Royce, W. C. Hocking, and even Hegel can be said to have propounded a form of self-realization theory. Although these men frequently disagreed, their quarrels were more like denominational feuds than religious wars and pointed out their similarities more than their differences.

They realized that the hedonistic theory of good fell short in that something could be pleasurable but not good and good but not pleasurable. When pleasurable states were called good it was by virtue of a wider value than pleasure. It was not enjoyment, then, which was the supreme good in life, but something more inclusive that could be identified with the individual's overall welfare. The good, it was decided, had to be a state in which people fully develop their various capacities, actualize their potentialities, and become all that they are capable of becoming. And this means not only fulfilling physical drives for food, sex, and property, which often seem the primary concerns of hedonism, but realizing the richer tendencies of one's nature as well. For example, a person's social tendencies would be realized, including the desire for the respect of others and the capacity for compassion. Also included in people's nature is an intellectual capacity that is expressed in the search for knowledge; a capacity for religious experience including awe, reverence, and solemnity before the universe; and an ability to appreciate beauty realizable in aesthetic contemplation and creation. All of these powers are inherent in the self and constitute what we term human nature as opposed to our animal nature.[6]

Since people can select between competing impulses rather than being at the mercy of a stimulus-response mechanism (i.e., action is possible, not just reaction), they are able to adjust their various impulses in the interest of the harmonious development of the entire personality. Lesser impulses can be subordinated to greater ones, the trivial to the profound, and life activities chosen relative to the end of complete self-realization. An ideal self can be projected imbuing existence with purpose and direction, and if people are deliberate and fortunate they will be able to maximize their selfhood in their lifetime, becoming their ideal selves.

Some theorists such as T. H. Green link the realization of the self to a concept of deity. God is that totality and completeness of being which the human spirit aspires toward, the perfectly realized entity, and therefore to approach one's ideal self is to approach the divine. Full realization means participation in eternal consciousness; God and man are united as in an apotheosis. This is a predictable extension of the theory once the notion of an ideal self is introduced, for a perfect spiritual being is its obvious end.

It is interesting to notice in passing that Sartre's distinction between "l'en soi," the in-itself or completeness of being, is only possible for objects: people, who are "le pour soi" or the for-itself, are always separated from completeness by a gap of consciousness. Human beings are aware of the world, and of themselves regarding the world, and this awareness implies a schism between subject and object which can never be bridged. For to bridge it would mean loss of consciousness, descent to the level of an object rather than a human being, and the absence of any awareness that one had achieved completeness of being. Although people are constantly aspiring toward this goal, it is logically self-contradictory and there is no danger of their ever achieving it.

But the telling criticism against the self-realization ethic is not an existentialist one—in fact, the two philosophies are mutually compatible.[7] The essential problem consists in the discrepancy that can exist between a realized self and what is good. For not all of human tendencies are good (to think otherwise is an act of faith, not a matter of fact), and a kind of self may be realized which is not good at all. Even if Genghis Khan were fully developed we would be hard-pressed to praise the result, and if it were argued that he developed his animal nature rather than his human nature, the problem would remain of differentiating between the two *descriptively*; relishing another person's suffering is as human as rejoicing at his good fortune. To separate the two *evaluatively*, that is, calling every good tendency human and every bad animal, is to present a circular argument which begs the question at issue.

A dilemma emerges then which appears inescapable. Either self-realization maintains that human nature should be fully realized, in which case good is not necessarily brought about, or the definition of good is qualified to something like "realizing that which it is good to realize," thereby involving a tautology. Like Mill, the self-realizationist stumbles over a necessary refinement with respect to higher and lower, which points beyond the theory itself for sanctions.

There are other theories such as stoicism and evolutionism that are in no way apologetic for our natural tendencies but, like Taoism, conceive of the good for human beings as conformity to that natural order of which we are a part. Whether nature is operating primarily within humans or outside, immanent or transcendent, its influence is salutary and not pernicious. In order to make this assertion credible, of course, certain metaphysical assumptions must be held.

The Stoic assumes that nature possesses a rational order and is moving intelligently and deliberately toward a good end. The universe may resemble a machine or a cabbage, the mechanical or the organic, but there is meaning throughout with intellect guiding and disciplining the whole. If people are to be moral and achieve the good, they must discern nature's inner principle and live in harmony with the purpose for which both they and the universe exist—an essentially beneficial purpose, despite appearances. Although nature may seem indifferent or malevolent, this judgment is more an indictment of human understanding than of nature itself. Both goodness and intelligence are at work, and the wise man actively cooperates with nature's order, never resisting any happenings in his lifetime, whether pleasant or painful, but always taking events as necessary and for the best. "Accept everything that happens, even if it seems disagreeable because it leads to this, the health of the universe," Marcus Aurelius writes. And the good for the universe is identical with the good for humanity.

Evolutionism is the more modern nature theory claiming that the type of evolutionary development operative throughout the universe furnishes a moral model for mankind. Good is defined teleologically as that end toward which the evolutionary process is moving; consequently our task and moral obligation consist in furthering the goal of complete evolvement. We must mime nature in her operations by creating a civilization that, according to Herbert Spencer at least, embodies the virtues of self-preservation, protection of the young, and social cooperation—"the greatest totality of life in self, in offspring, and in fellowman." Other evolutionary theorists, such as Sir Leslie Stephen, the Huxleys, Peter Kropotkin, among others, present variant values but hold in common that the evolved life is the ethically desirable life.

Both of those theories blatantly violate the "naturalistic fallacy" which logically prohibits the derivation of a value system from descriptive facts (including facts about nature), and for this reason are generally in disrepute among philosophers, although they do have some currency among laypeople. Periodically one hears "We must be philosophical," meaning Stoical about bearing suffering, or "It's survival of the fittest in this world," which is usually intended as justification for exploitation; however, the people who make these statements may not have reflected very deeply about them.

Various other conceptions of the good occur within ethics besides happiness, pleasure, self-realization, and conformity to nature's order or evolution, but those mentioned are major and representative ones.

THE RIGHT

Very often the notion of right will be linked to that of the good. Once the ultimate end of life has been determined, right can be defined as action that contributes to it, and wrong as that which opposes that end. Epicurus, for example, regards right actions as those that produce maximum pleasure for the individual, and Spencer discusses the "adjustment of acts to ends." However, a teleological mentality of this sort can be troublesome. In attempting to justify behavior through the moral consequences of an act, both the quality of the act and the motive of the agent can be neglected, and immoral actions condoned in terms of the moral end achieved. Acts that would ordinarily be considered wrong would then be called right because they produced the good, and this hardly seems defensible. In fortunate moments right and good coincide and moral choice involves relatively little deliberation, but there are occasions in which the two appear irreconcilable. Then the individual is forced to decide which is of primary importance: acting in the right way or realizing some good.

The list of right and wrong actions is comparatively short. Most ethicists have devoted their energies to justification for calling certain types of actions praiseworthy and others blameworthy rather than suggesting original definitions.

More exhaustive codes have been presented by various religions, for example, the Laws of Manu, the Ten Commandments, the Creed of Nanak, the Sermon on the Mount, and so forth. In both cases the "thou shalt nots" generally monopolize the list, which is unfortunate since not only do prohibitions create a taste for that which they prohibit, but they negate rather than affirm life. Perhaps the prevalence of negative rules is not so much an index of our tendency toward evil, which society is attempting to curb, as an indication of the enviousness, resentment, and joyless disposition of moralists.

These considerations aside, a set of rules typical to ethics would include moral injunctions against acts of murder, theft, adultery, and lying, and endorsement of such duties as keeping promises and paying debts. On a less specific level, being just or compassionate is sometimes considered right, or more basically still, acting wholly in accordance with what one judges to be a moral duty—a notion integral to Kantian ethics. Once a set of ethical rules is formulated, the individual is then called upon to observe its requirements with utmost stringency. The principles of right and wrong dictate what should be done, irrespective of the consequences to those affected by the action (including the agent). An unconditional and primary moral duty exists that constrains freedom within the bounds of responsibility.

When an individual who feels an obligation to behave according to certain ethical principles conflicts with a person whose behavior is directed toward securing the good, an interesting dilemma occurs. It is a dilemma of much greater subtlety than mere conflict between selfishness and altruism because both parties can be selfless in their attitudes, and it is not a straightforward collision of ethical beliefs, but a difference in kind between alternative approaches. The either/or question comes about because of differing moral perspectives.

To the academician a fascinating moral puzzle is then presented which requires clarification if not resolution. The writer on the other hand sees the dramatic potential of the situation: sincerity locked in combat with sincerity, a highly principled individual opposing a farsighted humanitarian, rigidity juxtaposed against compromise, dignity contrasted with concern, personal duty versus promotion of beneficial ends.

ANOUILH'S *ANTIGONE*

Jean Anouilh's play *Antigone* like all genuine art lends itself to diverse interpretations, but one valid explanation of the dramatic conflict is that Creon is effecting the good while Antigone is doing what is right, and in the situation presented the two are incompatible. The circumstances are as follows.

A clash occurs between Antigone and Creon over whether the body of Polynices, Antigone's brother, should be buried. Creon, the king, has decreed that Polynices' corpse is to remain on a hill, exposed to scavengers until it is consumed or it decomposes, because the youth died a traitor. Polynices had led a revolt against his brother Eteocles, with whom Creon had sided. The brothers killed each other in a civil war and Creon, who had ascended to the throne, declared Polynices anathema. He did this not because he was sincerely convinced that Polynices acted traitorously and Eteocles was innocent, but in order to intimidate all potential revolutionaries in the society. His motivation was to teach the rabble a lesson by having the stench of his rotting body fill the town; justice to the memories of the dead was of no concern. One brother is arbitrarily declared a loyal prince, the other a traitor; and it does not matter which is which because truth is not at stake, only the ordering of the population of Thebes. A hero and a villain are needed; the one to serve as a venerated martyr, the other as a criminal whose end is an awful warning against revolt.

"Well, what else could I have done?" Creon explains to Antigone.

> People had taken sides in the civil war. Both sides couldn't be wrong; that would be too much. I couldn't have made them swallow the truth. Two gangsters were more of a luxury than I could afford. . . . And this is the whole point of my story. Eteocles, that virtuous brother, was just as rotten as Polynices. That greathearted son had done his best, too, to procure the assassination of his father. That loyal prince had also offered to sell out Thebes to the highest bidder. Funny, isn't it? Polynices lies rotting in the sun while Eteocles is given a hero's funeral and will be housed in a marble vault. Yet I have absolute proof that everything that Polynices did, Eteocles had plotted to do. They were a pair of blackguards—both engaged in selling out Thebes, and both engaged in selling out each other; and they died like the cheap gangsters they were over a division of the spoils.
>
> But, as I told you a moment ago, I had to make a martyr of one of them. I sent out the holocaust for their bodies; they were found clasped in one another's arms— for the first time in their lives, I imagine. Each had been spitted on the other's sword, and the Argive cavalry had trampled them down. They were mashed to a pulp, Antigone. I had the prettier of the two carcasses brought in, and gave it a state funeral; and I left the other to rot. I don't know which is which. And I assure you, I don't care.[8]

This is probably the true story, but a truth that must never be told or acted upon for the good of society. Creon is adopting the theory of justice as a deterrent and not as a fair response to wrongdoing. Actual guilt does not matter. If it is politically advantageous to condemn one man and praise another, we have all the authority necessary: the larger good. Justice is designed to provide what is socially beneficial; if it proves harmful, then justice must be refashioned so that it serves society once more. Considerations as to the truth of accusations are petty scruples, militating against the general welfare. An instrumental totalitarian view of justice must be operative in which the individual's civil rights are far from sacred. Respect for honesty and fairness should be subordinate in importance to the salutary effects of the legal verdict. Since the societal value of conviction and punishment consists in their deterrent value to prospective criminals, the verdict and sentence are what matters and not their appropriateness to the facts.[9]

A flaw, of course, is that once individuals know that political exigencies and not guilt determine the decision of the authorities, they are no longer deterred from committing crimes. Whether people are lawbreakers or law-abiding citizens, they are equally liable to conviction. However, the system only collapses when people realize that justice, in its usual sense, has been abridged. All rulers adopting this ethic take great pains to keep this fact from the people—and Creon is no exception.

It is not that Creon is exploiting the credulity of the people for his personal benefit; it is for their own good. He is paternalistic, not selfishly despotic. The means he adopts are often repugnant to him, the stench of the rotting corpse is disgusting, and he despises the hypocrisy of solemn orations by old men to the memory of Eteocles. Nevertheless, he believes that the welfare of the state has moral priority over personal qualms and he does what is required. Ethical reservations are fine for adolescents but rulers cannot afford to be so naive or squeamish. Polynices must remain as he is, unburied and unmourned, despite the violence done to decency and integrity. To him, these are mere words, not realities. The survival of the society is at stake, which overrides all other considerations and reduces them to relative insignificance.[10]

By contrast, Antigone's perspective does not encompass concern for the ultimate good; practical ethics leave her unmoved. Considerations as to the consequences of action are thought to be extraneous and corrupting. Her temperament is not congenial to calculation or the deliberate pragmatism of the careerist or the diplomat. She does not weigh her actions for effect but acts in response to ethical demands which impinge upon her as personal responsibilities. Certain actions are right and should be done, regardless of the fact that they are absurd and pointless in the long run. The burial of Polynices is an obligation of this kind, and therefore all arguments that point out the futility of doing so do not touch her; they are beside the point.

After Creon upbraids and threatens her for attempting to bury Polynices, she starts to walk away, unimpressed by the king's rage.

> ANTIGONE. I must go and bury my brother. Those men uncovered him.
>
> CREON. What good will it do? You know that there are other men standing guard over Polynices. And even if you did cover him over with earth again, the earth would again be removed.
>
> ANTIGONE. I know all that. I know it. But that much, at least I can do. And what a person can do, a person ought to do.

The act will not accomplish anything worthwhile, but it is a moral obligation to which she should respond.

Usually if a person who proposes a course of action is shown that it will not produce the intended result and furthermore will incur a penalty of death, this is sufficient discouragement. But Antigone is stepping to a different drum and hearing music which is far away, as Thoreau says. Perhaps she is unreasonable, headstrong, and obstinate, but what Creon never fully understands is that Antigone's commitment to personally correct conduct is at stake, which is the basis of her self-respect. Creon persists in illustrating the absurdity of her cause, as though she were acting for the sake of some end.

CREON. Tell me, Antigone, do you believe all that flummery about religious burial? Do you really believe that a so-called shade of your brother is condemned to wander forever homeless if a little earth is not flung on his corpse to the accompaniment of some priestly abracadabra? Have you ever listened to the priests of Thebes when they were mumbling their formula? Have you ever watched those dreary bureaucrats while they were preparing the dead for burial—skipping half the gestures required by the ritual, swallowing half their words, hustling the dead into their graves out of fear that they might be late for lunch?

ANTIGONE. Yes, I have seen all that.

CREON. And did you never say to yourself as you watched them, that if someone you really loved lay dead under the shuffling, mumbling ministrations of the priests, you would scream aloud and beg the priests to leave the dead in peace?

ANTIGONE. Yes, I've thought all that.

CREON. And you still insist upon being put to death— merely because I refuse to let your brother go out with that grotesque passport; because I refuse his body the wretched consolation of that mass-production jibber-jabber, which you would have been the first to be embarrassed by if I had allowed it. The whole thing is absurd!

ANTIGONE. Yes, it's absurd.

CREON. Then why, Antigone, why? For whose sake? For the sake of them that believe in it? To raise them against me?

ANTIGONE. No.

CREON. For whom then if not for them and not for Polynices either?

ANTIGONE. For nobody. For myself.

Even if Antigone succeeded in burying her brother, she does not believe a sacred service will have been performed for the soul of Polynices, and the more Creon undermines her actions as fruitless, the more she discerns and confirms the ground for her behavior. If she is acting for anyone it is herself, meaning her fidelity to her conscience. This is why she falters but does not recant when Creon discloses the truth about the character of Polynices. She loses her faith, as she puts it, but gradually rallies her courage. The deeper reasons for her choice begin to reassert themselves, and the alternative is exposed in all its cheapness.

CREON. Go and find Haemon. And get married quickly, Antigone. Be happy. Life flows like water, and you young people let it run away through your fingers. Shut your hands; hold on to it, Antigone. Life is not what you think it is. Life is a child playing round your feet, a tool you hold firmly in your grip, a bench you sit down upon in the evening, in your garden. People will tell you that that's not life, that life is something else. They will tell you that because they need your strength and your fire, and they will want to make use of you. Don't listen to them. Believe me, the only poor consolation that we have in our old age is to discover that what I have told you is true. Life is nothing more than the happiness that you get out of it.

ANTIGONE. (Murmurs, lost in thought) Happiness . . .

CREON. (Suddenly a little self-conscious) Not much of a word, is it?

ANTIGONE. (Quietly) What kind of happiness do you foresee for me? Paint me the picture of your happy Antigone. What are the unimportant little sins that I shall have to commit before I am allowed to sink my teeth into life and tear happiness from it? Tell me: to whom shall I have to lie? Upon whom shall I have to fawn? To whom must I sell myself? Whom do you want me to leave dying, while I turn away my eyes?

CREON. Antigone, be quiet.

ANTIGONE. Why do you tell me to be quiet when all I want to know is what I have to do to be happy? This minute; since it is this very minute that I must make my choice. You tell me that life is so wonderful. I want to know what I have to do in order to be able to say that myself . . .

CREON. Be quiet, I tell you!

ANTIGONE. Why do you want me to be quiet? Because you know that I am right? Do you think I can't see in your face that what I am saying is true? You can't admit it, of course; you have to go on growling and defending the bone you call happiness.

The price Antigone must pay for doing what is right is high: nothing less than her life. But the price Creon pays for the good of happiness is even higher; he must forfeit his soul. In dedicating himself to happiness, above all else he must quash his sense of rightness and perpetrate any crime that expediency requires. And paradoxically, even though he is king, he is more limited in his actions than Antigone because he must act according to the good and never in opposition to it. He is not at liberty to do as he pleases but only as he must. His private principles and sentiments must be made subservient to the necessities of his position.

"I can say no to anything I think vile," Antigone taunts Creon, "and I don't have to count the cost." Creon cannot do anything without assessing its implications. At another point she tells Creon, "You are a loathsome man!" to which he replies, "I agree. My trade forces me to be." And elsewhere Antigone distinguishes their positions by saying, "I don't have to do things that I think are wrong . . . you didn't really want to leave my brother's body unburied, did you? . . . But you did it just the same. And now, though you don't want to do it, you are going to have me killed. And you call that being a king!"[11]

Yet Creon is not unequivocally the villain of the piece; he is acting strictly for the sake of the society and not for his own benefit. In a sense he is every bit as much a martyr as Antigone, even superior perhaps, for he devotes his life to humankind whereas she sacrifices herself to abstract principles. He would have preferred having a private and sedentary existence, indulging his interest in books, but he woke up one morning to find himself king of Thebes. To have refused the crown would have been a cowardly abdication of responsibility, particularly since the state was in imminent danger of foundering. "There had to be one man who said yes," he says.

> Somebody had to agree to captain the ship. She had sprung a hundred leaks; she was loaded to the waterline with crime, ignorance, poverty. The wheel was swinging with the wind. The crew refused to work and were looting the cargo. The officers were building a raft, ready to slip overboard and desert the ship. The mast was splitting, the wind was howling, the sails were beginning to rip. Every man jack on board was about to drown—and only because

the only thing they thought of was their own skins and their cheap little day-to-day traffic. Was that a time, do you think, for playing with words like *yes* and *no*? Was that a time for a man to be weighing the pros and cons, wondering if he wasn't going to pay too dearly later on; if he wasn't going to lose his life, or his family, or his touch with other men? You grab the wheel, you right the ship in the face of a mountain of water. You shout an order, and if one man refuses to obey, you shoot straight into the mob. Into the mob, I say! The beast as nameless as the wave that crashes down upon your deck; as nameless as the whipping wind. The thing that drops when you shoot may be someone who poured you a drink the night before; but it has no name. And you, braced at the wheel, you have no name, either. Nothing has a name—except the ship, and the storm.

By contrast, Antigone sometimes appears a self-indulgent, stubborn, and hysterical adolescent. She is described by the chorus in the introductory scene as "the tense, sallow, willful girl whose family would never take . . . seriously," and many of her speeches reinforce the image of a child lost in fantasy who refuses to accept adult reality. At points she is childlike in her purity and impulsiveness, at other times childish, but she seldom conducts herself maturely. Witness the following outburst:

I want everything of life, I do; and I want it now! I want it total, complete: otherwise I reject it! I will *not* be satisfied with the bit of cake you offer me if I promise to be a good little girl. I want to be sure of everything this very day; sure that everything will be as beautiful as when I was a little girl. If not, I want to die!

There is something commendable in her unwillingness to compromise with a vision of what life should be, whether dream or ideal; however, the overall impression is that of a spoiled child. When she repeatedly says "no," perhaps out of petulance, or, as a more serious charge can be leveled against her: she is confirming her identity by negating life. From this perspective Creon's "yes" signifies a healthy endorsement of existence, positive and embracing. Despite Antigone's speech to Ismene about being "the first out of bed because she loved the touch of the cold morning air on her bare skin," she only wants the image of life, the romantic fleeting moments of existence, more imagistic than real. Creon says yes to life in its concreteness, thereby accepting the repulsive with the delightful. His purpose in assuming the throne was to maintain life in being when it was threatened by disintegration, to reduce the chaos to order—the same order nature finds necessary to perpetuate its species. In his act of assent he is assisting life in its ongoing thrust and flow: as he says, only the ship and the storm have meaning.

Antigone defies him in the extreme, saying, "I am here to say no to you, and die," to which he replies,

It is easy to say no. To say yes, you have to sweat and roll up your sleeves and plunge both hands into life up to the elbows. It is easy to say no, even if saying no means death. All you have to do is to sit still and wait. Wait to go on living; wait to be killed. That is the coward's part. No is one of your man-made words. Can you imagine a world in which trees say no to the sap? In which beasts say no to hunger or to propagation? Animals are good, simple, tough. They move in droves, nudging one another onward, all traveling the same road. Some of them keel over; but the rest go on; and no matter how many may fall by the wayside, there are always those few left which go on bringing their young into the world, traveling the same road with the same obstinate will, unchanged from those who went before.

Do those who endorse principles deny life? Does preoccupation with ethics mean a rejection of existence? Are there spiritually minded souls who reside so completely within the realm of utopias, the city of God, that they can never accept the world as it is? Can people never again adjust their eyes to the gloom of earth after they have seen the light of stars? Is the kiss of Ondine or the swan fatal to contentment as a human being? Must we make a choice between this life and the ideal? Perhaps the two are incompatible, and Antigone is condemned to a tragic end because she chooses principles.

Creon believes this is the case, for he says to Antigone, "You come of people for whom the human vestment is a kind of straitjacket: it cracks at the seams. You spend your lives wriggling to get out of it. Nothing less than a cozy tea party with death and destiny will quench your thirst." And his summation of Antigone in the last act is that "Death was her purpose, whether she knew it or not. Polynices was a mere pretext. When she had to give up that pretext, she found another one. She was bent upon only one thing: to reject life and to die."

However, this judgment is not entirely fair. Antigone's purpose is to do what is right, and if this entails dying, then she accepts the penalty. The premium she places upon principles makes her depreciate the value of life, but she is not intent on death. The results of her actions must not be taken as her purpose.

After subtracting the weaknesses of Antigone's immaturity, there remains something fiercely noble in placing integrity above life itself, to act according to what is right and wrong, not helpful or harmful. Her attitude is reminiscent of Socrates in the *Crito* when he argues, "[T]he only question . . . is whether we shall do rightly [in escaping from prison] . . . or whether in reality we shall not do rightly: and if the latter, then death or any other calamity which may ensue on my remaining here must not be allowed to enter into the calculation . . . the really important thing is not to live, but live well."[12] One could also plead, as Sartre does, that people's dignity is founded on their capacity for holding certain values more important than death. When people can say "Rather death than . . . ," they have identified and asserted the grounds of their humanness.[13] On these terms, Antigone's uncompromising spirit places her among the elite of the earth.

Is Creon a callous tyrant, then, and Antigone a martyr to inviolable principles, or is Creon a realistic moralist plagued by an unreasonable girl? One's answer to this question largely depends upon whether the good or the right is considered more important—the good here interpreted by Creon as the happiness of the society, established in accordance with nature's orderly process, or the right conceived by Antigone as honoring ethical obligations at all costs. Anouilh has not solved the moral dilemma but he has dramatized it superbly.

TOLSTOY'S *ANNA KARENINA*

Anna Karenina involves the same dilemma although not as overtly. Tolstoy clearly intended right to triumph, not through militancy but by the hand of God. However, the moralist in Tolstoy warred incessantly with the artist. Consequently, the intention is never wholly realized in the literary work—which, aesthetically, is for the best. Gaps and holes are left through which the good can seep through as the more human response. A thoroughgoing didacticism tends to destroy art by treating it instrumentally, that is, as a vehicle for moralizing; plot, character development, and language are sacrificed to propaganda. Tolstoy by and large escapes this defect, as perhaps the plays of Camus and Shaw do not, by making all of his characters sympathetic, living creatures, including the most reprehensible ones. The moralist deliberately attempts to show how the wicked reap the wages of sin, but the artist educes our empathy and understanding, thereby engendering compassion. Severity is only possible when human beings are dehumanized as "the wicked" or "the enemy," otherwise the similarities between others and ourselves become too apparent and we are softened in our judgment. Occasionally a sympathetic portrayal of vice can overturn our customary assessment altogether and cause us to question our standards. Or more properly stated, we are led to wonder whether ordinary standards of conduct should give way before more human desires. Actions are then viewed in relation to both the needs of the heart and the demands of the head, which are often two magnetic poles with equal attraction.

Without completely intending to do so, Tolstoy generates this type of tension through the presentation of Anna Karenina's passion set against the respectability and ethicism of her husband, Alexey Alexandrovitch, and the virtues of Konstantin Levin. It is unintentional since Tolstoy wants to portray Anna's liaison outside marital bonds as inexcusable, both immoral and irreligious, but by creating Anna so lovingly our response is mixed, our loyalties confused and divided. Adultery is a sin, yet perhaps under certain circumstances, for particular persons and special reasons, to fulfill essential needs there are exceptions that escape absolute judgment. Adulterous conduct may never be commendable, but it might be immune from moral censure.

The book is long but the plot simple; that the novel is gripping is a tribute to Tolstoy's genius for vivid portraiture. Anna, the wife of a tedious but important government official, falls in love with a charming army officer named

Vronsky. She leaves her husband and child for him and ultimately commits suicide out of an acute sense of shame and sinfulness. As a family chronicle, other people's lives are involved, including Anna's brother, Stepan Oblonsky, and her sister-in-law, Dolly, who function in minor roles, and two more distant relatives, Kitty Schtcherbatsky and her husband, Levin, the latter occupying a major position in the story. The marriage of Kitty and Levin is favorably contrasted with that of Anna and Alexey, and Anna's tortured search is set off against Levin's satisfactions.

Levin is Tolstoy's mirror, his chosen son, the surrogate and proxy of his moral strivings. A landed noble like Tolstoy, he is most at peace in the country living close to the land and among the peasants, conscientiously managing his estate. His life is exceedingly rich within and without, full of plans and projects for the improvement of the farm and his own character. He tries to employ scientific principles of agriculture and has a theory that the character of the laborer on the land is as important to production as the soil or climate; to him, treating the peasant as an abstract force is simplistic and wrongheaded.

Levin theorizes from the midst of the peasants, not from an armchair. He is not treated as one of them but they are natural in his company and he is at home in theirs. Despite the irritation he sometimes experiences struggling with their carelessness and resistance to change, they evoke great sympathy within him; their wholesomeness duplicates his own. Stepan describes him as having "a true, honest nature, and a heart of gold," which are precisely the qualities he admires in his "souls."

On one occasion, ideal and paradigm, he mows the grass with the peasants, swinging a scythe all day in a long line of men, feeling purified by laboring over the land amidst simple people. Tolstoy writes,

He thought of nothing, wished for nothing, but not to be left behind the peasants and to do his work as well as possible. He heard nothing but the swish of scythes and saw before him . . . the crescent shaped curve of the cut grass, the grass and flower heads slowly and rhythmically falling before the blade of his scythe, and ahead of him the end of the row, where would come the rest . . . in spite of the sweat that ran in streams over his face and fell in drops down his nose, and drenched his back as though he had been soaked in water, he felt very happy.[14]

And when an old man offers him a drink of fresh water from a stream, Tolstoy declares, "And truly Levin had never drunk any liquor so good as this warm water with green bits floating in it, and a taste of rust from the tin dipper." Almost a mystical unity is achieved with humanity, sanctified by this communion; the water undergoes transubstantiation as wine, the blood of Christ.

Levin is also content in the company of children, playing foolish games and teaching them gymnastic tricks, and the children trust him unreservedly (as they do Anna): "[They] experienced in regard to him none of that strange feeling of shyness and hostility which children so often experience toward hypocritical, grown-up people." Tolstoy says and then adds, somewhat tritely, "Hypocrisy in anything whatever may deceive the cleverest and most penetrating man, but the least wide-awake of children recognizes it, and is revolted by it, however ingeniously it may be disguised. Whatever faults Levin had, there was not a trace of hypocrisy in him, and so the children showed him the same friendliness that they saw in their mother's face."

Children; healthy peasants; the pace, contours, and odors of the countryside; absorbed and cherished, have formed Levin's disposition and character. He lives according to the clean, natural laws imprinted by his surroundings, and finds cosmopolitan tastes mystifying. Tolstoy's own penchant for rural life and the morality of those close to the soil is represented through his preferences and aversions. The land can teach a man the value of mutual helpfulness for the benefit of all, and natural justice, for as one sows so shall he reap. It can show the preciousness of home and family as something earned through labor, and reproach dishonesty by compounding work postponed or neglected. Courage can be instilled through adversities of droughts, frosts, and floods; patience in the face of unalterable conditions; and all beneficial activities have their appointed time, set by the tempo of the seasons.

These are the lessons Levin has internalized and the outlook he carries within him whether in the country or the town. They are a set of homespun, simple virtues but, to Tolstoy's mind, closer to God's will than theories of ethics proposed by the urbane. Tolstoy was a sincere Christian, and for him Christianity is a gospel of salvation to the poor and humble, not the sophisticated. The intellect misleads people, and is cheating and deceitful. Right living comes about by following natural truths, not the ideas of philosophy.

As a consequence, Levin is always uncomfortable in the city. He cannot comprehend occupations like the civil service or finance; they seem artificial and oddly immoral by being unproductive. He enjoys clever conversation, but the urban intellectuals confuse him with their acute logic that often seems to skirt the real problems. Moving in city society even for a brief time upsets him and the return to the country is perceived as a deliverance. The following is typical of his reactions:

> In the morning Konstantin Levin left Moscow, and towards evening he reached home. On the journey in the train he talked to his neighbors about politics and the new railways, and, just as in Moscow, he was overcome by a sense

of confusion of ideas, dissatisfaction with himself, shame of something or other. But when he got out at his own station, when he saw his one-eyed coachman, Ignat, with the collar of his coat turned up; when, in the dim light reflected by the station fires, he saw his own sledge, his own horses with their tails tied up, in their harness trimmed with rings and tassels; when the coachman Ignat, as he put in his luggage, told him the village news, that the contractor had arrived, and that Pava had calved,—he felt that little by little the confusion was clearing up, and the shame and self-dissatisfaction were passing away. He felt that at the mere sight of Ignat and the horses; but when he had put on the sheepskin brought for him, had sat down wrapped up in the sledge, and had driven off pondering on the work that lay before him in the village, and staring at the side-horse, that had been his saddle-horse, past his prime now, but a spirited beast from the Don, he began to see what had happened to him in quite a different light. He felt himself, and did not want to be any one else. All he wanted now was to be better than before.

Even fine restaurants make him "sore and uncomfortable." They are places of frivolity and bustle, with private rooms where men dine with ladies; there are bronzes, mirrors, gas, and waiters, all of which is offensive. Dining one evening at such a place with Stepan he expresses his contempt for the useless elegance of the city:

"It's too much for me," responded Levin. "Do try, now, and put yourself in my place, take the point of view of a country person. We in the country try to bring our hands into such a state as will be most convenient for working with. So we cut our nails; sometimes we turn up our sleeves. And here people purposely let their nails grow as long as they will, and link on small saucers by way of studs, so that they can do nothing with their hands."

Stepan Arkadyevitch smiled gaily.

"Oh, yes, that's just a sign that he has no need to do coarse work. His work is with the mind . . ."

"Maybe, but still it's queer to me, just as at this moment it seems queer to me that we country folks try to get our meals over as soon as we can, so as to be ready for our work, while here are we trying to drag out our meal as long as possible, and with that object eating oysters . . ."

"Why, of course," objected Stepan Arkadyevitch. "But that's just the aim of civilization—to make everything a source of enjoyment."

"Well, if that's its aim, I'd rather be a savage."

Levin's plain values are often revealed in conversation with Stepan, who relishes the sensuous refinements of urban living to the point of being a voluptuary. Stepan says,

"Suppose you're married, you love your wife, but you're fascinated by another woman . . ."

"Excuse me, but I'm absolutely unable to comprehend how . . . just as I can't comprehend how I could not, after my dinner, go straight to a baker's shop and steal a roll."

". . . Why not? A roll will sometimes smell so good one can't resist it."

"What's to be done—you tell me that, what's to be done? Your wife gets older, while you're full of life. Before you've time to look round, you feel that you can't love your wife with love, however much you may esteem her. And then all at once love turns up, and you're done for, done for . . . But what's to be done?"

"Don't steal rolls."

". . . Oh, moralist!"

Much later, at Levin's estate, Stepan returns to the subject and the metaphor, but Levin again is unmoved.

"You don't admit, I know, that one can be fond of new rolls when one has had one's rations of bread—to your mind it's a crime; but I don't count life as life without love," he said, taking Levin's question in his own way. "What am I to do? I'm made that way. And really, one does so little harm to anyone, and gives oneself so much pleasure . . ."

"What! Is there something new, then?" queried Levin.

"Yes, my boy, there is! There, do you see, you know the type of Ossian's women . . . Women, such as one sees in dreams . . . Well, these women are sometimes to be met in reality . . . and these women are terrible. Woman, don't you know, is such a subject that however much you study it, it's always perfectly new."

"Well, then, it would be better not to study it."

"No. Some mathematician has said that enjoyment lies in the search for truth, not in the finding it."

Levin listened in silence, and in spite of all the efforts he made, he could not in the least enter into the feelings of his friend and understand his sentiments and the charm of studying such women.

Undeniably, Levin's innocence is overdone; Tolstoy's puritanism does intrude upon the narrative at times, particularly when he derides the pleasures of smoking, dancing, gambling, drinking, and music,[15] but also in his portrayal of Levin as insensitive to certain normal attractions. That which is sinful is not automatically unappealing; if it were there would be no victory in choosing good over evil. A man is usually commended for resisting temptation, not for being immune to it. But Tolstoy, in his eagerness to display a moral model, occasionally exaggerates his hero's purity, thereby reducing credibility and betraying literature. Happily, these lapses occur infrequently, for one is impressed overall with the strong realism of the characters. In fact, Tolstoy belongs to that genre of writers who reveal life more than they transmute life into art.

But Levin is portrayed as genuinely high-minded, an aristocrat with grassroot virtues, earnestly seeking the way through society's seductions to right thinking and right living. His social milieu prizes outward conformity to convention while disregarding genuine values, in fact, punishing sincerity that violates the forms of decorum. Levin's decisions flow from his conscience, not the expectations of his class, and although his logical faculties are not acute his instincts are sound. They conduct him beyond intellectualism to moral devotion. He follows principles from a sense of their natural rightness, thereby embracing a higher ethic. He does not articulate his code but nevertheless moves in response to its demands. More a moral being than a moralist, he is Tolstoy's vision of the Christian, implicitly obeying the righteous spirit within him.

Anna and Levin's stories run concurrently, touching now and again via common contacts, but whereas Levin's marriage fulfills him, Anna's husband represses her nature; she must seek fulfillment elsewhere. Under the same circumstances Levin would have conducted himself according to the marital rules as he indicated to Stepan, but Anna is made of different stuff, she follows her needs rather than her obligations. In Jung's terms, she is the completion-seeking female, not the perfection-seeking male, and thus pursues the good rather than the right.

To paint Anna, Tolstoy uses a special palette of language: "warmth," "elegance and modest grace," "charming face," "vigorous," "free," "the elasticity of her movements," "very beautiful," "a fully-developed figure lightly carried," "something peculiarly caressing and soft . . . in her expression," "a freshness and unflagging eagerness . . . in her smile and her glance," "perfectly simple and concealing nothing . . . [yet having] another higher world of interests . . . complex and poetic," a "suppressed eagerness which played over her face, and flitted between the brilliant eyes and the faint smile that curved her red lips. It was as though her nature were so brimming over with something that against her will it showed itself now in the flash of her eyes, and now in her smile."

The adjective "eagerness" recurs and implies a certain ardor and sensitivity, a visible longing to absorb life experiences and to give of herself from some rich wellspring within. It comes to suggest a deeply affectionate disposition, barely controlled and severely stifled, and an inextinguishable, unrealized capacity for love. She is brimming over with a womanliness and warmth that is anxious to be expressed instead of remaining latent or abstract.

This fundamental need to express and receive love has been thwarted in her marriage to Alexey Karenin, an arid bureaucrat twenty years her senior, a correct and dutiful man grossly deficient in humanity and romantic feeling. Tolstoy describes him as having "lived and worked in official spheres, having to do with the reflection of life. And every time he stumbled against life he had shrunk away from it." Vronsky has "a vague recollection of something stiff and tedious evoked by the name Karenina," someone "clever, learned, religious somewhat."

The marriage, arranged by an aunt when Anna was too young, is an obvious mismatch; the contrast between husband and wife is extreme and mutually impoverishing. After more than eight years of emotional deprivation and tedium, Anna meets Vronsky, a man called by Stepan "one of the finest specimens of the gilded youth of Petersburg. . . . Fearfully rich, handsome, great connections, an aide-de-camp, and with all that a very nice, good-natured fellow." Vronsky's character is not ideal by any means, but he is more worthy of Anna than Karenin ever could be, and he offers Anna the romantic and passionate love essential to her.

A classic situation thus exists which in more enlightened times might have ended in divorce, but given the rigid norms of St. Petersburg it must end tragically; no resolution is possible within the rigid social structure. To remain with Karenin would be intolerable for Anna once she has known love, and to live with Vronsky, as she decided to do, proves equally devastating. Ecclesiastical law prohibits remarriage while the husband is living, therefore divorce would never legitimize their relationship. Vronsky tries to shoot himself, but even if he had succeeded in taking his own life Anna's happiness would not have been secured. If Karenin had committed suicide Anna would then have borne the stigma of the woman who had driven her husband to his death. Escape is impossible for her, except in fantasies and dreams.

After being with Vronsky, Anna attempts to return to normal marital relations, but dissatisfaction with Karenin gives way to repulsion at his approach. Tolstoy reports that at the sight of her husband "the eagerness dies out of her face, and when he tries to touch her, her first impulse was to jerk back her hand from the damp hand with big swollen veins." During this period Anna confesses to Stepan,

> I can't live with him. Do you understand? The sight of him has a physical effect on me, it makes me beside myself. I can't, I can't live with him. What am I to do? I have been unhappy and used to think one couldn't be more unhappy, but the awful state of things I am going through now, I could never have conceived.

Karenin's words do almost less for his cause than his person, for he is only concerned with the social embarrassment that Anna's behavior causes him. He tells her, "I consider jealously, as you know, a humiliating and degrading feeling, and I shall never allow myself to be influenced by it; but there are certain rules of decorum which cannot be disregarded with impunity."

"He doesn't care," Anna thinks. "But other people noticed . . . and that's what upsets him." When he speaks of love, Anna wonders, "Love? Can he love? If he hadn't heard there was such a thing as love, he would never have used the word." Not even Karenin's eventual self-abasement makes him any less despicable in her eyes. Even if they had been compatible initially, the relationship could never be restored after all that had transpired.

Anna therefore chooses the alternative of an illegitimate liaison with Vronsky, but her situation is hopeless. Abroad they live like exiles or fugitives from respectable society, and back in St. Petersburg Anna is exposed to insults and humiliation. Under these conditions, Vronsky's love for Anna cools. He begins to feel that she inhibits his freedom while she in turn grows possessive and irritable, jealous of every woman and desperate at the decrease of his love. Quarrels break out at the slightest provocation, exasperation occurs on both sides, weariness, petty revenges, recriminations, and finally hatred. Anna's character deteriorates to the level of her role as mistress, and the world appears vile and hateful to her eyes. In a state of self-disgust and loathing for life, she hurls herself under the wheels of a train.

Because Anna degenerates so radically toward the end, our respect for her diminishes and is replaced by pity for her torment. Yet her situation is to blame; it is totally impossible. If there had been socially acceptable means to realize her desires, she would never have been reduced to degradation. More important, the fact that Anna came to a bad end might not prove the wrongness of her decisions. To Tolstoy the consequences of action have nothing to do with their morality, in fact, he has Levin state, "If goodness has causes, it is not goodness; if it has effects, a reward, it is not goodness either. So goodness is outside the chain of cause and effect."

In the same way, Levin is an unalloyed hero not only

because he finds a rewarding life, but because he also does the right things—particularly in contrast to the likeable but lecherous Stepan. Yet by the same token, Anna emerges superior to her husband, Karenin; compared to his punctiliousness her vitality and yearnings are like sunshine to stone. Or to alter the perspective, Karenin is the perversion of Levin's moral posture while Anna's need for love is distorted in Stepan. The real issue, then, is choosing between Anna and Levin: Anna's desire for self-realization and happiness through love (a definition of the good), or Levin's adherence to principles above all else (a choice of the right).

As in the case of Creon and Antigone, a logical disjunction is posed between the good and the right with no hope of passing between the horns of the dilemma. If Anna's mode of realizing herself and achieving happiness is considered misguided, Levin's standards can be judged to be unsatisfactory as well. Levin champions the orthodoxies absorbed with his mother's milk, as he says, which is not the most promising approach to independent truth, and he would maintain these without compromise even at the expense of a good life. Luckily, the conflict does not arise for him, but he clearly endorses the right over the good. Anna pursues the good, which for her necessarily involves love, and she persists in her aim despite the violence done to rightness and the rules of marriage.

We cannot even turn to pragmatic considerations for resolution because Levin prospers through following what is right and Creon prospers doing what is good. Conversely, Anna ruins herself struggling for the good while Antigone is destroyed adhering to what is right. To base our choice on what promotes life in particular circumstances is merely to expose our values rather than to solve the problem.

The ethical problem therefore remains with its ambiguities, nuances, and subtleties exposed in effective literature.

NOTES

1. There are other moral senses of "good" as in "good character" and "good as a means" which will not be considered here. I am concerned with "the good," which I would take to be the primary usage in ethics. Nonmoral uses of good include: "Good burglars are quick and quiet," "Chocolate is good but spinach is good for you," "Jean Genet is a good writer," "Generals rarely have good ideas," etc.

2. For an interesting and responsible popularization of the *Nicomachean Ethics*, see Henry Veatch's *Rational Man* (Bloomington: Indiana University Press, 1962). James Walsh's book *Aristotle's Conception of Moral Weakness* (New York: Columbia University Press, 1963) provides good insight into Aristotle's ethical theory and, of course, W. D. Ross's *Aristotle* (London: Methuen, 1964) is an outstanding general commentary.

3. For a sympathetic study of the Epicurean philosophy by a superb stylist, see Walter Pater's *Marius the Epicurean* (New York: Dutton, 1934).

4. Philosophy was never a matter of dry cerebral contemplation among the early Greeks but a source of delight and adventure. Edith Hamilton quotes the beginning of Plato's *Protagoras* as typical of Greek liveliness. Socrates is awakened at dawn by a hammering at his door: "'What's here?' he cries out, still half asleep. 'O Socrates,' and the voice is that of a lad he knows well, 'Good news, good news!' 'It ought to be at this unearthly hour. Well, out with it.' The young fellow is in the house now. 'O Socrates, Protagoras has come. I heard it yesterday evening. And I was going to you at once but it was so late—' 'What's it all about—Protagoras? Has he stolen something of yours?' The boy bursts out laughing. 'Yes, yes, that's just it. He's robbing me of wisdom. He has it—wisdom, and he can give it to me. O come and go with me to him. Start now.'" See all of chapter 2 in *The Greek Way* (New York: W. W. Norton, 1930): it is overly lyrical but haunting nonetheless.

5. Walls are ambiguous things just as pleasure has its posi-

tive and negative aspects. I might add that the negativism of Epicurus has a parallel in the silver rule of the Old Testament: "Do *not* do unto others what you would *not* have them do unto you." The Christian version is positive, of course, which is not to say superior. It is an open question whether helping people is better than leaving them in peace.

6. Throughout history various facets of the prism have been presumed to be human nature. Humans have been labeled the political or social animal, the rational being, the only creature who destroys his own kind, the tool-using animal, the only animal capable of being dissatisfied (Don Juan being the symbol of eternally dissatisfied man), the language-using animal, and the only creature who eats when he isn't hungry, drinks when he isn't thirsty, and makes love all year round. (This last characterization is used by Beaumarchais in *Le Mariage de Figaro*, but it has an earlier, anonymous source.) The descriptions usually stress either man's unique abilities or his outstanding ones, and sometimes resemble caricatures more than characterizations. Aristotle went wrong in assuming that rationality is the only characteristic unique to human beings.

7. What the existentialist calls the essence of humans (which is created subsequent to existence by decisions and actions), the self-realizationist refers to as actualized potentialities. These terms are perfectly harmonious and are central to each philosophy.

8. J. Anouilh, *Antigone*, trans. Galantiere, in *Four Contemporary French Plays* (New York: Random House, 1967). This source is used throughout.

9. Strangely enough, both totalitarianism and extreme liberalism are prone to contempt for truth in their conceptions of justice. The liberal tends to reject the punitive theory which is based upon the desire for revenge, and advocates instead that criminals be treated with regard to their eventual rehabilitation, the protection of society, and deterrence of others. But logically this implies that no connection need exist between crime and the verdict of a court. On this theory an innocent person could be judged guilty

and incarcerated if he or she were considered in need of rehabilitation and society would profit from the example. Crime might be considered an index of that need but not necessarily the only index. The new theories of penology, for which Warden Lewis Lawes was the spokesperson, suffer from this theoretical defect.

10. There is a marvelous passage in which Creon compares his practicality with the anguish of Oedipus, Antigone's father:

> Don't think that being a king seems to me romantic. It is my trade; a trade a man has to work at every day; and like every other trade, it isn't all beer and skittles. But since it is my trade, I take it seriously. And if, tomorrow, some wild and bearded messenger walks in from some wild and distant valley—which is what happened to your dad—and tells me that he's not quite sure who my parents were, but thinks that my wife Eurydice is actually my mother, I shall ask him to do me the kindness to go back where he came from: and I shan't let a little matter like that persuade me to order my wife to take a blood test and the police to let me know whether or not my birth certificate is forged. Kings, my girl, have other things to do than to surrender themselves to their private feelings.

And more seriously he tells her, "Let me tell you Antigone: those days are over for Thebes. Thebes has a right to a king without a past. My name, thank God, is only Creon. I stand here with both feet firm on the ground; with both hands in my pockets; and I have decided that so long as I am king—being less ambitious than your father was—I shall merely devote myself to introducing a little order into this absurd kingdom; if that is possible."

11. It is worth noticing that although Antigone despises Creon, she needs him as an opposing force just as extraordinary people need ordinary people for differentiation. Alceste in *Le Misanthrope*, who is a blood relative to Antigone, recognizes that we cannot all be ethically fastidious. "If everyone were clothed with integrity, if every heart were just, frank, kindly, the other virtues would be well

nigh useless since their chief purpose is to make us hear with patience the injustice of our fellow." And one of the criticisms of Kant's theory, that genuine morality is universalizable, is that some virtues are impossible to universalize, for example, if everyone is self-sacrificing, there is no one left to accept the sacrifices.

12. In this section of the *Crito* (48E) Socrates antedates Christ in his assertion that if something is wrong it should never be done—not even when one is wronged. "One ought not to return a wrong or an injury to any person, whatever the provocation is."

13. See Sartre's *The Republic of Silence.*

14. L. Tolstoy, *Anna Karenina,* trans. Constance Garnett (New York: Fine Editions Press, 1946). All quotations from *Anna Karenina* are taken from this edition.

15. The novel is honeycombed with subtle condemnations of this type. For example, Stepan asks Levin, "How is it you don't smoke? A cigar is a sort of thing, not exactly a pleasure, but the crown and outward sign of pleasure." Tolstoy does not intend such considerations as recommendations. And after Vronsky has spent an evening in a wholesome household, he carries away an "exquisite feeling of purity and freshness, and debates where next to go: "'Club? A game of bezique, champagne with Ignatov? No, I'm not going. Chateau des Fleurs; there I shall find Oblonsky, songs, the cancan. No, I'm sick of it. That's why I like the Schtcherbatskys', that I'm growing better. I'll go home.' He went straight to his room at Dussots' Hotel, ordered supper and then undressed, and as soon as his head touched the pillow, fell into a sound sleep." This is obviously the sleep of the blessed who have a clear conscience.

3

THE PROBLEM OF EVIL

Goethe's *Faust*, Dostoevsky's *The Brothers Karamazov*, and Voltaire's *Candide*

*A*ccording to doctrine, God is the supreme being, the creator, sustainer, and lord of the universe. Human beings perceive in themselves a suggestion of the wisdom that deity possesses, an echo of his power, a trace of his goodness—all distorted and perverted by original sin. God's actual omniscience, omnipotence, and omnigoodness, as well as other perfections, are virtually inconceivable. They can be approached only obliquely and negatively, through hints and flashes, in poetry and mystical awareness. To attribute to God anything but positive characteristics indicates a failure in comprehension and a blasphemous departure from the creed sanctified by martyrs and codified by Schoolmen. As an eternal being we must regard God as beyond all temporal dimension, present everywhere and always, boundless and changeless, encompassing everything and lacking nothing. As an omnipresent force he must be thought immanent as well as transcendent, perpetually available to respond to prayers and intervene in human affairs, redressing wrongs and righting moral imbalance, constantly operating upon our spirit and within our conscience. As a God of love he is exhaustively concerned with the well-being of his children and in providing a world in which goodness triumphs.

A profound problem exists, however, in reconciling a deity of these proportions with the evil that human beings confront as part of their given environment. What explanation can there be for earthquakes, volcanoes, and hurricanes if God is wholly benevolent? How can we account for killing cold and burning heat, poisonous insects and reptiles, leukemia, multiple sclerosis, and heart disease, and the disfigurement of aging? When one considers the sufferings inflicted upon humankind by centuries of disease and countless catastrophes, it is hard to exonerate God much less praise him.

To be more precise, we have four classes of evil that we confront: natural disasters, hostile environments, sickness and disease, and old age and death. The nature of the universe and the nature of deity therefore seem logically incompatible. If God is unable to prevent natural evil, he cannot be omnipotent; if he is unaware of it, he cannot be thought omniscient; and if he is unwilling to alleviate pain, he cannot be judged omnigood. Without an adequate explanation we must either renounce belief in God or maintain that he creates only to torture and destroy.

The technical name for this issue is "the problem of evil," which is trying to harmonize God's love, power, and wisdom with the fact of human suffering. In a polytheistic system the dilemma does not arise. Certain of the gods can be thought malevolent, perpetually at war with mortals and their gods of the pantheon. The Egyptian god Set, the Vedic Rudra, and many of the gods of primitive peoples, including the Maori, the Santal of India, the Koksoagmiut Eskimos, and the Gold Coast tribes of Africa, function in precisely this way; all evil events are attributed to their influence. No thought is given to praise of these deities, only the offering of chants, charms, and incantations to propitiate their wrath.

The dilemma is also rendered irrelevant if we conceive of a dualistic universe bifurcated into good and evil forces as in Zoroastrianism where Ahura Mazda and Angra Mainyu battle for cosmic supremacy. Although people might suffer in this cosmology, there is an explanation of the suffering. The existence of natural evil implies an inconsistency only when all events, the harmful as well as the helpful, are attributed to a single, supreme deity.

SUFFERING IS PUNISHMENT FOR SIN

One alleged solution to the problem claims that human beings deserve the punishment they receive—and perhaps a good deal more. Adam and Eve tasted the forbidden fruit in Eden, and all humanity inherited that original sin. We are still succumbing to temptation daily, continuing to rebel against God's will. Human sinfulness has not abated through the years but has only been compounded, often in subtle ways. Whereas battleaxes and maces formerly were used to wound and kill, we now employ chemical, biological, and nuclear weapons as instruments for our crimes. Whereas in former times when cities were defeated the men were killed and the women and children sold into slavery, today missiles annihilate everyone indiscriminately. Greed previously bred larceny and expansionism; now it causes water and air pollution, threatening the extinction of all life. Everywhere one looks the earth is ripe with violence, selfishness, and horror, *omnia contra omnes*, a perpetual conflict of opposites and contraries. At one moment people are concerned with their own advantage, at another they adopt awful means for effecting altruistic ends. If the world is so constituted that sin prevails, then small wonder that God punishes humankind using the natural evils at his disposal. A just God could do nothing else.

We often see the universe operating precisely in this way, producing harm as a natural consequence of immoral or thoughtless actions. Overeating strains the heart and excessive drinking weakens the liver; smoking causes cancer and sexual promiscuity can lead to a social disease; neglected wounds become septic and neglected crops wither; untested ice drowns skaters and untended dikes allow floods to consume homes. Since lapses in duty or attention often incur painful results in a natural cause-effect sequence, it seems reasonable to magnify this relationship to cosmic dimensions and assume that God has a retributive scheme in operation. He rewards virtue and castigates vice, meting out just desserts via the medium of natural evil. If we suffer some misfortune, an appropriate question seems to be, "What have we done to deserve this punishment?"

However, although such a response is common, it does not seem logically valid. For evil people do not necessarily suffer, any more than the good always prosper. Evil does not fall on all the wicked or on only the wicked, but acts more like rain, falling on the just and the unjust alike. And those who most deserve punishment often receive it least, while those who deserve it least are buried beneath an avalanche of calamities. In short, the distribution is askew as well as the amount of suffering relative to the degree of sinfulness. When a house is struck by lightning and burns to the ground, we cannot say that only sinners have been consumed, and when a ship sinks in a storm, the passengers and crew are not ipso facto evil. Conversely, those individuals who escape disaster all their lives do not necessarily deserve to lead charmed lives; some awful people have amazing luck.[1]

Undeserved suffering is, of course, the theme of the book

of Job in which disaster is piled upon disaster for an individual described as "blameless and upright, one who feared God and turned away from evil." Through no fault of his own Job loses his children, servants, and livestock, and then is afflicted with an awful disease. The moral quality of his life simply does not justify punishment of this depth and breadth, yet he suffers more than the most depraved person. And the pain inflicted upon him certainly cannot be justified in the way proposed within the book of Job, namely, as the outcome of a contest between God and Satan over Job's faithfulness to God. To test a person's faith by killing his family is far too gruesome a *means* to be morally permissible. Therefore, we do not accept this explanation as acquitting God but, if anything, as an additional reason for questioning his character. The statement "Though he slay me yet will I trust him" may reflect a noble attitude of faith but, in a logical sense, a god who permits slayings is not the sort to be trusted or worshiped.

The problem of evil, then, is not solved by Job, but rather the alleged solution of natural evil punishing moral evil is aired and found wanting: Job is a paradigm, contrary case.

EVIL TESTS OUR FAITH

Variations upon the theme of humans being tested through suffering occur in Goethe's *Faust*, except that here the trial is by temptation rather than misfortune. The same duel occurs between God and the devil over a man's soul, the same contest over loyalties as in Job, but for Faust evil comes in the guise of an invitation to experience the totality of the universe. To accomplish the same end the devil chooses a different instrument, assuring Faust of extraterrestrial knowledge without restriction.

To win his wager with God, the devil offers to conduct Faust on a fabulous tour through all the realms of reality, and Faust for his part is prepared to violate sacred precincts and sell his very soul to see beyond the screen of human understanding. Quite willingly he is seduced into exploring the supernatural and unnatural spheres, the sacred as well as the profane. He consents to hold no area of experience forbidden or inviolate, nothing sacrosanct or prohibited by reason of its holiness, and no bargain too dear for unrestricted breadth of knowledge.

In the "Prologue in Heaven," Mephistopheles meets with the Lord and the motive for the temptation of Faust is made explicit:

MEPHISTOPHELES.
Since you, O Lord, once more draw near and ask how all
is getting on . . . Of suns and worlds I've naught to say worth
mention. How men torment them claims my whole
attention. Earth's little god retains his same old stamp
and ways
And is as singular as on the first of days.
A little better would he live, poor wight,
Had you not given him that gleam of heavenly light.
He calls it Reason, only to pollute
Its use by being brutaler than any brute.
It seems to me, if you'll allow, Your Grace,
He's like a grasshopper, that long-legged race
That's made to fly and flying spring
And in the grass to sing the same old thing.
If in the grass he always were reposing!
But in each filthy heap he keeps on nosing.

THE LORD.
You've nothing more to say to me?
You come but to complain unendingly?
Is never aught right to your mind?

MEPHISTOPHELES.
No, Lord! All is still down right bad, I find.
Man in his wretched days makes me lament him;
I am myself reluctant to torment him.

THE LORD.
Do you know Faust?

MEPHISTOPHELES.
The Doctor?

THE LORD.
Yes, my servant!

MEPHISTOPHELES.
He! Forsooth, he serves you most peculiarly.
Unearthly are the fool's drink and his food;
The ferment drives him forth afar.
Though half aware of his insensate mood,
He asks of heaven every fairest star
And of the earth each highest zest,
And all things near and all things far
Can not appease his deeply troubled breast.

THE LORD.
Although he serves now confusedly,
I soon shall lead him forth where all is clear.
The gardener knows, when verdant grows the tree,
That bloom and fruit will deck the coming year.

MEPHISTOPHELES.
What will you wager? Him you yet shall lose,
If you will give me your permission
To lead him gently on the path I choose.

THE LORD.
As long as on the earth he shall survive,
So long you'll meet no prohibition.
Man errs as long as he doth strive.

MEPHISTOPHELES.
My thanks for that, for with the dead I've never
Got Myself entangled of my own volition.
I like full, fresh cheeks best of all the lot.
I'm not at home when corpses seek my house;
I feel about it as a cat does with a mouse.

THE LORD.
'Tis well! So be it granted you today!
Divert this spirit from its primal source
And if you can lay hold on him, you may
Conduct him downward on your course,
And stand abashed when you are forced to say:
A good man, though his striving be obscure,
Remains aware that there is one right way.

MEPHISTOPHELES.
All right! But long it won't endure!
I have no fear about my bet, be sure!
When I attain my aim, do not protest,
But let me triumph with a swelling breast.
Dust shall he eat, and that with zest,
As did the famous snake, my near relation.

THE LORD.
In that too you may play your part quite free;
Your kind I never did detest.
Of all the spirits of negation
The wag weighs least of all on me.
Mankind's activity can languish all too easily,
A man soon loves unhampered rest;
Hence, gladly I give him a comrade such as you,
Who stirs and works and must, as devil, do
But ye, real sons of God, lift up your voice,
In living, profuse beauty to rejoice!
May that which grows, that lives and works forever,
Engird you with Love's gracious bonds, and aught
That ever may appear, to float and waver,
Make steadfast in enduring thought![2]

Faust appears easy prey to Mephistopheles because of his insatiable spirit, his restlessness, and his longing for universal comprehension and, above that, universal experience. He is straining at the limitations imposed by the human state, by being confined to animal perceptions and earthly knowledge. He is precluded by the restrictions of corporeality from realizing and becoming everything, and by the constructions of logic from attaining the impossible. Science, the arts, and even the black arts offer an inverted telescope of reality, schemes, and architectonics that condense and diagram rather than render the deeper universe immediately available. Only direct involvement with the whole of life, the inner dynamic flux as well as the forms and appearances, can satisfy his high ambitions. And because he hungers so deeply for totality of being, he derides moral restraints upon the means of the search, and disparages theological distinctions between proper and improper realms for human exploration. Filled with wonder more than awe, the cosmos draws him forward and all barriers to satisfaction are swept aside; in short, he is ripe for hubris and tragedy.

The devil knows his victim, and knows, too, that the disillusionment Faust feels with being earthbound will extend to the supernatural once that has been attained. Then, having forfeited his soul, Faust will find he has only deepened his despondency, for even the transcendental will turn to ashes in his mouth. Having braved hell, he will discover nothing novel beyond this world, nothing so rapturous as to make eternal torment bearable. Totally disillusioned, he will be grateful even for dust.

If Faust had submitted to utter despair, Mephistopheles would have won his wager. Faust does experience disenchantment but at the final moment his spirit revives and is transfigured by understanding. He realizes that dissatisfaction is endemic to the attainment of all objectives, however exalted, but that perpetual striving and perpetual disappointment is itself the highest mode of living. To be discontented, to strive, to fail, and to pursue the unsatisfying again is the process whereby existence is justified and redeemed.[3] This is the wisdom which Goethe teaches and the grounds for Faust's salvation, for because his spirit is ultimately undefeated, his soul is born to heaven by angels chanting,

> Lo! Rescued is this noble one
> From evil machination;
> Who e'er aspiring, struggles on,
> For him there is salvation.
> And if to him Celestial Love
> Its favouring grace has given,
> The Blessed Host comes from Above
> And welcomes him to Heaven.

It is difficult to overpraise this moving and profound tale as literature or philosophy. However, the problem of evil is neither addressed nor solved by Faust's unwitting fulfillment of God's will. We cannot praise a divinity for deliberately testing a man through either suffering or temptation; a loving god does not deliberately thrust snares in a person's path or use a human being as a pawn to win a game. Although people may be praiseworthy for resisting temptation, that does not justify throwing temptation in their way. A parent who entices a child to sin is either malicious or misguided, and this approach is not validated by rewarding the child for being strong.[4] A god who uses such negative means, even for a worthwhile end, cannot be considered just.

Of course, the evil that Faust experiences is a special kind and not the sort that primarily interests us in the problem of (natural) evil. Whatever one thinks of God's motives here, the essential issue of theodicy concerns cases where people suffer without good reason. With regard to this dilemma, *Faust* is silent.

EVIL IS NECESSARY AS A CHOICE

The idea of resisting evil has generated a more sophisticated explanation for the existence of suffering in the world. Some theologians have claimed that evil must be present otherwise the choice of good would not be praiseworthy. That is, to make God's gift of free will meaningful and a moral victory, evil is essential as a choice for humankind. It would be senseless to endow people with the capacity for freedom and not give them the option of evil as well as good. Free will would exist in name only if good alone existed as the object of choice. Evil, therefore, must be present as a possibility if people are to be free and either praised or blamed for their decisions. Evil, then, is necessary evil, necessary to the meaningfulness of man's volition, and since we prefer free will to determinism, we should be prepared to accept evil as an essential condition.

Among religionists this explanation has some currency; nevertheless, serious problems appear once we analyze it. One difficulty pertains to the scale and depth of natural evils; they appear to be far in excess of that required to make choice meaningful. For instance, a certain number of diseases might be necessary to provide an opportunity to discover cures and alleviate suffering, but there is no need for a superabundance of diseases and of such a horrible nature. The common cold might be justified under this logic, but not tuberculosis, arthritis, meningitis, leprosy, typhus, and cancer; the medical textbook surely does not have to be so thick.

Furthermore, when evils strike choice is seldom possible. The avalanche buries the victim alive, the hurricane sweeps him away, the fire consumes him without providing an opportunity to say yes or no. There is no option offered between blindness and sight for the person born blind; and if the argument claims that moral opportunities are then available for others, it is hard to rejoice at the fact. A god with all means at his disposal could have arranged the universe differently so that the suffering of some people would not be the necessary condition for the free choice of others.

Philosophers have also pointed out that evil need not be present for freedom and responsibility to exist. A choice among good, better, and best is as free and moral as that between good and bad. Furthermore, the least good does not become bad relative to good, better, and best. Filet mignons are not as good as chateaubriand steaks, but they are not bad; ptomaine poisoning is bad.

Assuming that evil is necessary to be genuine, we must then ask whether free choice is sufficiently valuable to justify suffering. Perhaps freedom should have been sacrificed for the sake of peace and well-being.

Authoritarian individuals would certainly answer affirmatively with regard to the family and government. If the welfare of society and individual freedom is incompatible, then freedom becomes expendable, for freedom is not an ultimate end but a means, and if it proves counterproductive, then there is no justification for its retention. To defend that which entails torment and has no intrinsic merit is pure perversity. For the sake of human welfare perhaps people cannot be free.

This is the issue discussed in Dostoevsky's *The Brothers Karamazov* in the section titled "The Grand Inquisitor." Here Ivan rejects as intolerable any scheme that necessitates suffering, particularly the suffering of innocent children, even if the harmony of the universe is thereby achieved. And when his brother Alyosha introduces the concept of Christ's atonement as expiation, Ivan attacks the ministry of Christ from a humanistic standpoint. He argues that precious few people can endure, much less derive happiness from, the freedom of choice that Christ preached.[5]

Christ offered people the choice of either accepting or rejecting God without summoning spectacular supernatural events to impress them. He asked of them that they base their lives on an invisible and intangible God. He wanted them to believe in a being wholly transcendent and incorporeal, accessible only to those who repent their sins and commit themselves without secure knowledge. Instead of miracles, he offered them a narrow path to a distant heaven, and instead of dispelling doubts by plain assurances, he taught indirectly in parables, comprehensible only to those earnestly in search of God.

In the poem that Ivan recites to Alyosha to justify his position, the Grand Inquisitor had imprisoned Christ after he inexplicably appeared in Seville during the time of the Spanish Inquisition, "when fires were lighted every day to the glory of God, and in the splendid *auto-da-fé* the wicked heretics were burnt." Ivan describes how Christ had moved through the humid streets of the southern town silently "with a gentle smile of infinite compassion," stirring the people's hearts and drawing them to him irresistibly. Everyone recognized him. He cured a blind man who cried, "O Lord, heal me and I shall see thee," and raised a child from the dead on the steps of the Seville cathedral. At this point the cardinal, the Grand Inquisitor, observes him and orders that he be seized by the holy guard. Like the centurions before them, the guard do not refuse to obey the order. The crowd bow to the Grand Inquisitor's will, and Christ is again taken prisoner.

The Grand Inquisitor subsequently visits Christ in the palace prison and delivers a diatribe against him that constitutes the heart of the allegory. He charges Christ with having offered human beings not happiness but freedom, which is unbearable to most people who are "weak, vicious, worthless, and rebellious." Therefore, despite Christ's professed love for the world, he acted as though he did not love man at all; although he became mortal to sacrifice himself for humankind, in effect, he proved to be a malefactor not a benefactor. Faithful to God, he mistreated humankind; acting out of purity he insisted on that which would make people unhappy. He had ignored "admonitions and warnings," the three temptations of the devil (that "wise and mighty spirit") which would have established an infallible basis for human happiness. Instead of accepting the devil's wisdom and human well-being, Christ chose to preach the free choice of God.

The first temptation is paraphrased by the Grand Inquisitor as follows:

> Thou wouldst go into the world, and art going with empty hands, with some promise of freedom which men in their simplicity and their natural unruliness cannot even understand, which they fear and dread—for nothing has ever been more insupportable for a man and a human society than freedom. But seest Thou these stones in this parched and barren wilderness? Turn them into bread, and mankind will run after Thee like a flock of sheep, grateful and obedient, though forever trembling, lest Thou withdraw Thy hand and deny them Thy bread.[6]

But Christ refused to deprive people of freedom and to buy their obedience with bread; he had replied that man lives not by bread alone, thereby consigning humankind to misery. "Thou didst promise them the bread of Heaven," the Grand Inquisitor charges, but "can it compare with earthly bread in the eyes of the weak, ever sinful and ignoble race of man? And if for the sake of the bread of Heaven thousands and tens of thousands shall follow Thee, what is to become of the millions and tens of thousands of millions of creatures who will not have the strength to forego the earthly bread for the sake of the heavenly?"

By not choosing "bread" he was dividing humanity, not unifying it under a common belief. He deliberately failed to satisfy the universal and everlasting craving for a god. "So long as man remains free he strives for nothing so incessantly and so painfully as to find someone to worship," the Grand Inquisitor asserts. "But man seeks to worship what is established beyond dispute, so that all men would agree at once to worship it. For these pitiful creatures are concerned not only to find what one or the other can worship, but to find something that all would believe in and worship; what is essential is that all may be *together* in it. This craving for *community* of worship is the chief misery of every man individually and of all humanity from the beginning of time."[7]

The devil next tempted Christ to hurl himself from the pinnacle of the temple to prove his divinity is a dramatic gesture "for it is written: The angels shall hold him up lest he fall and bruise himself, and Thou shalt know then whether Thou are the Son of God and shalt prove then how great is Thy faith in Thy father." But Christ refused to "enslave man by a miracle"; he wanted man's faith free and unprejudiced, "not the base raptures of the slave before the might that has overawed him for ever."

However, the majority of people lack Christ's strength; the human race is not divine. Their natures demand supernatural events to sustain their belief, in fact, "when man rejects miracle he rejects God too; for man seeks not so much God as the miraculous." Christ had made the mistake of overestimating man's will and his fastidiousness. "By showing him so much respect," the Grand Inquisitor asserts, "Thou didst, as it were, cease to feel for him, for Thou didst ask far too much from him—Thou who hast loved him more than Thyself! Respecting him less, Thou wouldst have asked less of him. That would have been more like love, for his burden would have been lighter."

By refusing to cast himself down, Christ had rejected "miracle, mystery and authority," the three forces that would have captivated the conscience of man and liberated him from the torment of decision. Nothing causes suffering more than freedom of conscience, the Grand Inquisitor declares, but "instead of giving a firm foundation for setting the conscience of man at rest for ever, Thou didst choose all that is exceptional, vague and enigmatic: . . . In place of the rigid ancient law, man must hereafter with free heart decide for himself what is good and what is evil, having only Thy image before him as his guide. . . . Instead of taking men's freedom from them, Thou didst make it greater than ever! Didst Thou forget that man prefers peace, and even death, to freedom of choice in the knowledge of good and evil?"

In the third temptation, "all the kingdoms of the earth" were offered to Christ, absolute sovereignty over the earth, but Christ chose the Lord over both the world and Satan in his faithfulness to the will of heaven. "Why didst Thou reject that last gift?" the Grand Inquisitor challenges. "Hadst Thou accepted that last counsel of the mighty spirit, Thou wouldst have accomplished all that man seeks on earth—that is, someone to worship, someone to keep his conscience, and some means of uniting all in one unanimous and harmonious ant heap, for the craving for universal unity is the third and last anguish of man."

People have a psychological and metaphysical need to organize into a worldwide state—a need which Christ in his purity refused to satisfy. Throughout history people have been guilty of complicity with their Tamerlanes and Caesars, Alexanders and Napoleons, for these conquerors expressed the universal striving for unity and subjugation. Like Plato's guardians ruling the polis (as reason controlling the person), these men brought peace to people's troubled spirits, ordering the turbulence of diverse strivings to harmony and solidarity.

But Christ in his nobility said, "you shall worship the Lord your God and him only shall you serve," thus renouncing that reign over the earth which would have united men under a theocracy. He chose to given man what he should have rather than what he wanted or needed as a weak being. By denying man's desire for agreement and belonging, Christ again showed himself to be man's malefactor, sacrificing human well-being to God's will.

The church has assumed responsibility for correcting Christ's mistakes; it has allied itself with the devil in the interest of humanity. Rather than dismissing the virtues of bread, a secure conscience and unity because of their source or impurity, the church has adopted all of the means Christ rejected and, in the name of Christ, utilized them for human good. Instead of fostering freedom the church has striven to secure happiness, and has enslaved people in order to provide this happiness incompatible with freedom.

Christ had said man lives not by bread alone, but the church replies, "Feed men, and then ask of them virtue! When men are hungry there is no crime and therefore no sin." The Grand Inquisitor tells Christ that the church offers men food and not freedom, and being more realistic and humane, this approach will win the allegiance of mankind. "In the end (men) will lay their freedom at our feet, and say to us, 'Make us your slaves, but feed us.'" And by choosing bread they will have chosen a common object of worship through the beneficent medium of the church.

In its earthly wisdom the church also accepted the second temptation and appropriated responsibility for man's religious and moral decisions, thus relieving people of the awful burden of private conscience. Through miracle, mystery, and authority men have been awed into unquestioning belief and need not suffer the agonies of free choice. And people rejoice at being led like sheep; they feel immense gratitude toward the church for acknowledging their feeble nature and sanctioning some degree of sin as a normal consequence of human weakness.[8]

And the final temptation, that of unity and world domination, was also embraced to soothe the perpetual discord and disruption of life caused by diverse governments. "Just eight centuries ago," the Grand Inquisitor says, "we took from him what Thou didst reject with scorn, that last gift he offered Thee, showing Thee all the kingdoms of earth. We took from him Rome and the sword of Caesar, and proclaimed ourselves sole rulers of the earth . . . we shall triumph and shall be Caesars, and then we shall plan the universal happiness of men."

In response to this harangue, Christ says nothing but softly kisses the Grand Inquisitor on his aged lips. The old man shudders but does not recant. He opens the cell door and tells Christ to be on his way and never come back; for if he returned, he would only interfere with the work of the church.

A brilliant story and one of the finest specimens of Dostoevsky's genius, but how valid is the charge? According to standard interpretations, Dostoevsky is parodying the Catholic Church and communism, both of which are believed to annihilate freedom for the sake of communal happiness. Furthermore, Alyosha takes the "poem" as being in praise of Jesus, not as criticism of him. However, Dostoevsky often presented positions which he himself did not accept with such logical force that they became convincing. For example, Raskolnikov's justifications for murdering the pawnbroker woman in *Crime and Punishment* appear so persuasive that they subvert Dostoevsky's intention to present him as a negative example. This is due in part to Dostoevsky's own vacillation between submission to God and defiance of religious and moral codes. In fact, in the margin of his notebook, next to one of Raskolnikov's speeches, he wrote, "Devil take it! This is partly right." Perhaps a similar ambiguity pertains in "The Grand Inquisitor" and we simply must judge the issue without firm knowledge of Dostoevsky's purposes.

Even then, intention does not affect evaluation; arguments must be assessed on their own merits. Does freedom preclude happiness? Is happiness only possible when freedom has been surrendered? If so, then freedom is not necessarily a blessing and cannot be considered justification for physical evil; people would be enduring pain for the sake of that which brought unhappiness.

Although it is undeniably true that the anxiety generated by free choice often militates against happiness, and, as Sartre says, freedom can be regarded as a burden to which we are condemned qua human beings, nevertheless higher happiness seems impossible without it. The state of happy subjection idealized by the Grand Inquisitor refers to food, comfort, shelter, security, and the like; it does not include the higher modes of happiness associated with achievement, friendship, creativity, generosity, and the like, all of which require freedom. For these higher states, freedom does appear antagonistic to happiness; deeper human happiness appears accessible only when freedom is present.[9] Or to make the point from a different perspective, when happiness is conceived more as fulfillment and gratification, and less as pleasure and enjoyment, then freedom becomes a necessary condition for its realization. One cannot imagine a person who is enslaved being profoundly happy.

The criticism of freedom, therefore, has only limited force in that most men do not aspire toward higher happiness. Overall, then, freedom appears a mixed blessing when viewed from a historical rather than a theoretical standpoint, occupying an ambivalent position in relation to happiness. The fact that freedom is not an unqualified good may render it dubious as justification for the existence of natural evil.

GOOD REQUIRES EVIL

In addition to the argument that moral evil requires natural evil as punishment, and man's freedom demands it, the claim is sometimes made that the existence of natural good demands natural evil as a balance; if we are to have the one we must have the other as a logical concomitant. The form of this argument varies, but an assumption of universal necessity can be discerned as the common denominator.

One variety stresses destruction as the opposite side of creation, pain as the price of pleasure, ugliness as necessary for beauty, and darkness as preparatory for the light. The former elements are conceived as being temporally causal, or metaphysically related to the latter, and in all cases the sets are logically linked. For example, the Jewish apologist Moses Maimonides, after reflecting upon the problem of evil, declared, "Genesis can only take place through destruction, and without the destruction of the individual members, the species itself will not exist. Thus the true kindness, beneficence, and goodness of God is clear. He who thinks that he can have flesh and bones without being subject to any external influence, or any of the accidents of matter, unconsciously wishes to reconcile two opposites, viz., to be at the same time subject and not subject to change." This approach is closely paralleled in late Hinduism through the concept of the god Shiva (the Vedic Rudra) who is thought both "the threatener, the slayer, the vexer and the afflictor," as well as the creator, the auspicious one, and life energy. Shiva destroys in order to create, for death is merely the prelude to new forms of life in the biological cycle. Within the context of reincarnation it is a necessary condition for the emergence of new life. Sir Charles Eliot in his *Hinduism and Buddhism* describes the idea as follows:

> As a . . . philosophy, Shivaism possesses truth and force. It gives the best picture . . . of the force which rules the universe as it is, which produces and destroys, and in performing one of these acts necessarily performs the other, seeing that both are but aspects of change. . . . The Creator is also the Destroyer, not in anger but by the very nature of his activity. . . . The egg is destroyed when the chicken hatched; the embryo ceases to exist when the child is born; when the man comes into being, the child is no more.

The pre-Socratic philosopher Heraclitus (527–475) is the earliest philosophic source for the doctrine although he is concerned with cosmology more than the philosophy of religion, and emphasizes the fact of contrariety and change. Heraclitus maintained that without opposing forces, continually antagonistic and perpetually balanced, the universe could not exist. The opposition between heat and cold creates the seasons, just as the backward and forward movement of the taut wood propels the arrow from the bow. Tension enables the lyre to produce music, and sickness and labor make health and relaxation pleasant. Unless alternation occurs (including alteration between desirable and undesirable events), the world could not be maintained in being.

Interestingly enough, Heraclitus included such items as sickness and health in his list, thereby crossing the boundary between the metaphysical and epistemological, and introducing another variety of the argument. As an epistemic point theologians and philosophers have sometimes asserted that men would be unable to *appreciate* the good unless evil were experienced as a contrast. Not that good could not exist without corresponding evil, but that it would not be known as good. Contrasts are necessary for appreciation, it is asserted, to provide reference points in terms of which evaluations can be made, for how could we know the sweet without the bitter, prosperity without poverty, pleasure without pain? Evil, therefore, is necessary if we are to enjoy the good things; elimination of suffering means elimination of happiness and the reduction of the quality of life to an undifferentiated grayness.

On the assumption that this is correct, men such as John Calvin have argued further that the evils on earth not only render man capable of appreciating earth's blessings but also serve as negative inducements for attaining the perfect good of heaven. Human beings would never strive for heaven unless the world was "hellish," but would rest content with earthly pleasure, desiring nothing more than mortal life. God, comprehending this, deliberately introduced physical suffering and mental torment so that man would hold the earth in contempt and turn his thoughts toward heaven as spiritual release from the ills of the flesh. In contrast to worldly existence heaven will appear infinitely desirable, a paradise worth the sacrifices, discipline, and renunciations that Christianity demands.

To criticize the last-mentioned, epistemological variety of the argument first, it is not at all certain that men are so constituted that they need to experience the bad in order to appreciate the good. Surely strawberries could taste good to a person who has not tasted vinegar or castor oil, and sheer animal good health could be relished without the contrast of illness. Perhaps good things are appreciated more fully when one has experienced the opposite, but the argument does not claim that; in any case, it would hardly be a viable excuse for disasters and awful diseases, which provide too much of a contrast. As the argument stands, the reasoning seems highly dubious, for good things (including highly good things such as love and beauty) can be appreciated in the absence of their opposites.[10]

The only legitimate application of the statement "contrasts are necessary for appreciation" occurs when "contrasts" is defined as "noticeable difference" rather than "opposite," for it could be argued that some relative standard must be utilized for evaluation to occur. But even if this were granted, the implication is that greater and lesser *goods* must exist, not evils.

Calvin's argument, too, is here undercut, for it is based upon a fraudulent epistemic claim. People can appreciate and aspire toward heaven without experiencing hell on earth. We could be drawn forward by desire, by the carrot and not the stick. At best men would be less impatient to reach heaven if pain were not dogging their steps like Furies, but a loving God should be willing to accept this condition and relieve people of their physical torments. Positively put, only a malevolent God would force men to suffer so that they would long for release more fervently.

Another problem inherent in the argument of logical necessity pertains to all varieties of the argument and strikes nearer to the core: although one may speak about logical necessities with regard to propositions, it is incorrect to refer to logical necessities (or impossibilities) in nature. If all crustaceans have shells and lobsters are crustaceans, then necessarily lobsters have shells. This is an unavoidable truth of Aristotelian logic. However, there is nothing in the physical universe that must exist as it does; empirical states are contingent, and necessity is not applicable to them. This includes natural evil that cannot be said to exist by logical necessity. We need not have death as a prelude to life, individual destruction in order for the species to exist, opposition or oscillation for the proper balance of the universe. The world is under no logical compulsion to be organized in a particular way. And surely a benevolent God, who is supremely wise and possesses unlimited power for affecting his will, could have arranged the universe without including natural evil. He could also have organized human psychology so that neither differences nor opposites would be necessary for appreciation, thereby eliminating even the less good.

The argument is, in fact, invalid except in a formal, linguistic sense that is too trivial to offer much support. It does remain undeniable that "good" is meaningless without "bad" in the same way that "up" is meaningless apart from "down," that is, when conceived as a relational term. But that has nothing to do with good or evil in the actual world.

Probably no other novelist deals as directly with the problem of evil as Voltaire in *Candide*, and he is specifically concerned with the argument of logical necessity as proposed by Shaftesbury and Pope in England, and, more importantly, by Liebniz in Germany. Each of these men in their individual ways had championed an optimistic view of life in which negative events were considered required for the harmonious composition of the universe. That evil seemed unnecessary and superabundant was a reflection of our finite perspective rather than an indictment against God. Everything contributes to the ultimate good, and if men have not sufficient vision to understand why suffering is sometimes required, they simply must trust in the infinite wisdom and goodness of God. This is the philosophic burden of Pope's "Essay of Man," which accords with Shaftesbury's views:

> All nature is but Art, unknown to thee;
> All Chance, Direction which thou canst not see;
> All Discord, Harmony, not understood;
> All partial Evil, universal Good:
> And, spite of Pride, in erring Reason's spite,
> One truth is clear, WHATEVER IS, IS RIGHT.

There are obviously serious difficulties in the blind faith aspect of this argument, for if human beings are precluded by their limitations from judging evil as genuine evil, they are equally precluded from judging good as genuine good. God cannot be identified as either benevolent or malevolent, and optimism is as groundless as pessimism. The argument, in fact, is an instance of a fallacy called the *argumentum ad ignorantiam*: we cannot judge, therefore we know "X" is the case. But all that can be inferred from "we do not know" is "we do not know"; negative premises cannot yield positive conclusions.

Be that as it may, Voltaire was more interested in the claim of necessity in the argument, particularly as formulated by Leibniz. In his *Theodicy* Leibniz had reasoned that since we are finite creatures, deficient in manifold ways, we will inevitably involve ourselves in sinfulness. Through lack of compassion for our fellow humans, ignorance regarding circumstances or consequences, an inability to enact our principles, and so forth, humankind will commit sins; our very nature entails it. A world of finite creatures, then, is a world of sinful creatures. This being the case, punishment must be administered, and this God does through natural evils. But God allows only the precise amount of evil required to punish sinfulness and not a jot more. Consequently it can be asserted that this is the best of all possible worlds—a world with the minimum amount of evil possible given the quantity of sin that exists. Justice therefore prevails.

Voltaire found this rational proof ludicrous in the face of real suffering; it glossed over horror with cheap apologetics. He might have pointed out that people should not be punished for that which they cannot avoid doing, but he chose to launch a satirical attack upon the notion that this is the best of all possible worlds. By describing in literary form the full catalogue of man's miseries, he hoped to reduce the optimism of Leibniz to absurdity, and by the accuracy of his thrusts and a piercing wit he largely achieved his aim.

The impetus for his attack was supplied by the Lisbon earthquake of 1755 in which tens of thousands of people lost their lives. After a period of genuine brooding and despair over the event, Voltaire wrote his poem the "Désastre de Lisbon," and when Rousseau criticized the philosophic content of the poem in an extensive and celebrated letter, Voltaire replied with *Candide, ou l'Optimisme*.[11]

To make his point Voltaire has Candide, a gullible boy steeped in the optimistic philosophy of Leibniz, travel over the entire Western world experiencing moral and physical evil in countless varieties. As personal victim, eyewitness, or privy to the tales of others, he is exposed to thievery, murder, rape and disfigurement, wars, persecutions and *autos-da-fé*, earthquakes, diseases, storms at sea, and the ravages of old age. Everywhere men are slaughtering each other or are being slaughtered by nature in some calamity or other. If the stake and scaffold are not claiming their lives, then the plague is rotting their bodies. And at every opportunity Voltaire is quick to point out the moral. Witness the following description of a battle.

> Nothing could be smarter, more splendid, more brilliant, better drawn up than the two armies. Trumpets, fifes, hautboys, drums, cannons formed a harmony such as has never been heard even in hell. The cannons first of all laid flat about six thousand men on each side; then the musketry removed from the best of worlds some nine or ten thousand blackguards who infested its surface. The bayonet also was the sufficient reason for the death of some thousands of men. The whole might amount to thirty thousand souls. Candide, who trembled like a philosopher, hid himself as well as he could during the heroic butchery.
>
> At last, while the two kings each commanded a Te

Deum in his camp Candide decided to go elsewhere to reason about effects and causes.

Candide is baffled, for the facts do not fit his concept of the best of worlds. He wonders what the worst must be like, but he keeps his faith, having been indoctrinated in optimism by his tutor, Dr. Pangloss—a caricature of the German metaphysician. Pangloss taught a positive teleology that is garbled to the point of burlesque, "[T]hat things cannot be otherwise, for, since everything is made for an end, everything is necessarily for the best end." "Nothing exists in vain or without good purpose" . . . "noses were made to wear spectacles; and so we have spectacles. Legs were visibly instituted to be breeched, and we have breeches . . . as pigs were made to be eaten, we eat pork all the year round; consequently . . . all is for the best."

No matter what catastrophes occur, Pangloss persists in his philosophy, using bizarre arguments such as "private misfortunes make the public good, so that the more private misfortunes there are, the more everything is well." When a virtuous man is thrown off the ship on which Pangloss and Candide are sailing during a violent storm, Pangloss proves that the sea route to Lisbon had been expressly created for the man to be drowned in, therefore, all is as it should be. While he is proving this *a priori* the ship sinks, downing everyone except Candide, Pangloss, and a villainous sailor. To compound the disaster, shortly after they are washed up in Lisbon an earthquake shakes the city and thirty thousand of the inhabitants are crushed to death under the ruins of houses. But Pangloss assures everyone that "things could not be otherwise. . . . [A]ll this is for the best; for, if there is a volcano at Lisbon, it cannot be anywhere else; for it is impossible that things should not be where they are; for all is well." Even after a multitude of horrors have befallen Pangloss, he still maintains his first opinion, for to retract his ideas would be inconsistent and therefore conduct unbecoming a philosopher.

Needless to say, no one else in the novel shares his viewpoint. All of the people Candide encounters, from monks to kings, are complaining and cursing their fate. Nobody is happy; each new acquaintance has a more pitiable tale of woe than the last. And the misfortunes Candide experiences himself hardly generate an optimistic outlook. Gradually, as Candide suffers blow after blow, he loses his illusions entirely, and when someone asks him, "What is optimism?" he replies, "Alas! . . . it is the mania of maintaining that everything is well when we are wretched."

Voltaire's conclusion, however, is not a pessimistic one. Life is not good but it is not bad either: it is tolerable. Although fortunate happenings are rare, they do occur, and people do sometimes treat one another compassionately and honestly. Admittedly, the human condition largely consists of misery, but there are moments of peace and pleasure. Furthermore, our existence can be improved. If everyone would only apply themselves to human betterment in their own personal way, then everyone's happiness would be increased. It is only when we rely on philosophic theories that trouble arises, for then we are prone to accept the most absurd notions, contradicting the facts of experience. Using systems of thought, we try to justify awful actions for the sake of some long-term good, doing the worst things for the best reasons. "Il faut cultiver notre jardin," Voltaire concludes, and by the exhortation "We must cultivate our garden" he does not mean that we ought to withdraw from the world, but rather that we must strive to improve the lot of man through individual action on a modest scale. Natural evil cannot be eliminated but by the wise use of our powers areas of the earth can be shielded and cultivated.

By contrasting the rationalistic theory of Leibniz with empirical reality, Voltaire rebuts this version of the logical necessity argument. When viewed against the brute facts of human suffering, the excuse for evil becomes outrageous or downright silly. Like all satirists Voltaire exaggerates, but the point remains even after the excesses have been scraped away. In effect, Candide gives the coup de grâce to the logical necessity argument.[12]

SUFFERING IS CHARACTER-BUILDING

Our final answer to the problem of evil should be mentioned, for it reflects a view that is widely held and deeply felt: that suffering and hardship improve character. Consequently, natural evil is justified as a necessary condition for our moral betterment. It is asserted that people who undergo severe or prolonged pain develop dimensions to their personalities which the individual living in continual bliss can never hope to attain. Pain is purifying and disciplining. It refines our sensibilities, orders our will, and engenders a more reflective attitude of mind. Soft conditions tend to produce soft people—dissolute, spineless, and ineffectual. Inhospitable conditions create a challenge. We must canalize our energies to overcome threats to our existence, and in overcoming obstacles, the advancing glacier, woolly mammoth, Nile flood, and so forth, we improve ourselves together with our environment. Languishing in the Land of the Lotus Eater, we would never have become a superior species, but presented with real or potentially harmful occurrences we have gathered our strength and transcended our history. The same law which governs the production of great art and athletic achievement is operative in the development of human character; namely, that accomplishment must always be preceded by great struggle. If we submit and relax all of our lives in a comfortable environment, the world's work would never get done. Human beings would never develop their potential.[13]

The belief that suffering builds character has nearly attained the status of proverbial wisdom, and it is reflected in several literary works, including Tolstoy's *The Death of Ivan Ilvitch*, Knut Hansun's *Growth of the Soil*, and Shakespeare's *King Lear*. It is also developed in Machiavelli's *Discourses* and Hegel's *Philosophy of History*. Nevertheless, the validity of the thesis is highly questionable. If it is true that soft conditions produce soft people, then it is equally true that harsh conditions will produce harsh people; brutal conditions, brutes. In other words, the inference is specious. Even if people are made stronger by undergoing "the purifying flame of suffering," they are not necessarily made better, that is, morally finer.

In point of fact it is highly doubtful whether increased strength generally results at all, for people are more often demoralized by suffering than tempered by it; their confidence in their power and their hopeful attitude toward life can be irreparably undermined. Too many people have been debased by suffering rather than elevated by awful experiences to trust its salutary powers. Platitudes notwithstanding, stumbling blocks are not always stepping stones, problems opportunities, or obstacles challenges.

What's more, many outstanding people throughout history have developed good characters without enduring afflictions, which implies that evils are not required for character development—the central assumption of the argument.

It should also be mentioned that those persons who might have profited from overcoming obstacles have not always had them thrust in their paths, whereas those who needed pain least have sometimes suffered the most. As in the argument that evil is punishment, the distribution seems askew.

Theological justification, therefore, cannot be gained by reference to this argument any more than through the ones previously discussed. Too many difficulties arise for any of the "answers" to be judged valid. The problem of evil, then, remains a problem. It continues to nag the believer and arms both skeptics and cynics with ammunition for attacking the existence of God. For if when God's in his heaven all's right with the world, then when all's not right with the world perhaps God's not in his heaven.

On a conceptual plane thinkers sometimes speculate as to whether the dilemma constitutes a revelation by its very paradoxicality or exposes a total absurdity, whether it points beyond reason to a universe wider than logic or simply dredges to light a contradiction between God's attributes and the world he created.

We shall let the knight in Chaucer's *Canterbury Tales* have the last (quizzical) word, even though a definitive answer would be far more satisfying than an unresolved question. Our exasperation and bafflement is expressed here rather wryly; people with acute sensitivity to human suffering can react much more bitterly.

> What management is in this prescience
> That, guiltless, yet torments our innocence?
> And this increases all my pain, as well,
> That man is bound by law, nor may rebel,
> For fear of God, but must repress his will,
> Whereas a beast may all his lust fulfill.
> And when a beast is dead, he feel no pain;
> But, after death, man yet must weep amain,
> Though in this world he had but care and woe:
> There is no doubt that it is even so.
> The answer leave I to divines to tell,
> But well I know this present world is hell.

NOTES

1. The persistence of this "answer" despite its rational absurdity can be attributed to psychological factors: it satisfies our desire for explanation thereby keeping the unknown and mysterious at bay, and it does so in a way that expiates our pathological guilt; our sins are punished and our conscience is cleansed. Theologians for their part welcome this notion as providing a deterrent (just as hell is the ultimate deterrent); every disaster becomes an object lesson. Jesus generally rejects the idea that sin causes suffering, for example, John 9:1–3, although he hedges a bit in Luke 13:4–5.

2. J. W. Goethe, *Faust*, trans. G. M. Priest, in *Great Books of the Western World*, vol. 47, ed. R. M. Hutchings (Chicago: Encyclopædia Britannica, 1941).

3. In the *Myth of Sisyphus* Camus makes a similar statement in terms of fruitless, repetitive labor. Sisyphus has been condemned to the endless task of rolling a rock to the summit of a mountain from which it will immediately roll down. Sisyphus triumphs insofar as he accepts meaningless daily existence, thereby transcending despair and affirming life.

4. Another literary presentation of the temptation idea occurs in "The Friar's Tale" in Chaucer's *Canterbury Tales* where the yeoman, who is a devil, delivers the following speech to the summoner:

> Well, sometimes we are God's own instruments
> And means to do His orders and intents,
> When so He pleases, upon all His creatures,
> In divers ways and shapes, and divers features.
> Without Him we've no power, 'tis certain,
> If He be pleased to stand against our train.
> And sometimes, at our instance, have we leave
> Only the body, not the soul, to grieve;
> As witness Job, to whom we gave such woe.
> And sometimes have we power of both, you know,

That to a man which gives his soul unrest,
And not his body, and all is for the best.
And when one does withstand all our temptation,
It is the thing that gives his soul salvation;
Albeit that it was not our intent
He should be saved; we'd have him impotent.

And, of course, the plot of Milton's *Paradise Lost* pivots upon the devil's temptation and man's consequent fall. An interesting question here is whether Eve was seduced into sin by the serpent or the apple.

5. The problem Ivan confronts differs from the problem of evil in this respect: the evil discussed is moral evil, man's inhumanity to man, and the freedom is man's freedom to do evil (or good). Ivan is not concerned with the justification of natural evil as a condition for free choice. However, the worth of freedom is questioned relative to the pain that follows, and this question is relevant whether the pain is inflicted by man or nature.

6. The definitive translation by Constance Garnett is used here.

7. The Grand Inquisitor goes on to say, "For the sake of common worship they've slain each other with the sword. They have set up gods and challenged one another, 'Put away your gods and come and worship ours, or we will kill you and your gods!' And so it will be to the end of the world, even when gods disappear from the earth; they will fall down before idols just the same." This seems a more persuasive explanation of group conflicts and wars than saying that man is forever motivated by economic gain or is an aggressive animal by nature.

8. The following passage relating to sin and the church is particularly pointed and forceful:

Oh, we shall allow them even sin, they are weak and helpless, and they will love us like children because we allow them to sin. We shall tell them that every sin will be expiated, if it is done with our permission, that we allow them to sin because we love them, and the punishment for these sins we take upon ourselves. And we shall take it upon ourselves, and they will adore us as their saviours who have taken on themselves their sins before God. And they will have no secrets from us. We shall allow or forbid them to live with their wives and mistresses, to have or not have children—according to whether they have been obedient or disobedient—and they will submit to us gladly and cheerfully. The most painful secrets of their conscience, all, all they will bring to us, and we shall have an answer for all. And they will be glad to believe our answer, for it will save them from the anxiety and terrible agony they endure at present in making a free decision for themselves. And all will be happy . . .

. . . Peacefully they will die, peacefully they will expire in Thy name, and beyond the grave they will find nothing but death. But we shall keep the secret, and for their happiness we shall allure them with the reward of heaven and eternity.

9. Some philosophers, notably the existentialists, would maintain that if happiness and freedom are incompatible, then so much the worse for happiness; they would rather be free human beings than happy animals.

10. Additionally, the evils that exist are more numerous and severe than are necessary to provide a contrast; if we need a rainstorm to appreciate sunshine, we surely do not need floods, and influenza would be sufficient to make us appreciate health; we need not have cancer.

11. Various influences for *Candide* have been traced to the *Cosmopolite* of Fougeret de Monbron, Johnson's *Rasselas*, and Candido in Dekker's *The Honest Whore*.

12. Voltaire's general religious position was a deism shading, perhaps, to atheism.

He regarded God as some eternal geometer who had arranged matter according to certain universal laws and then abandoned it to run on unattended—an absentee landlord view. Voltaire's God, further, is finite in power, circumscribed by various limitations including that of his own nature.

13. On the strength of this notion ascetics and romantics alike have simulated natural hardships in their lives in the belief that achievement requires that people be miserable. It is also sometimes suggested as the secret of the English national character. G. B. Shaw writes, "An Englishman thinks he is moral when he is only uncomfortable."

SELF, MIND, AND BODY
Kafka's *Metamorphosis* and Rilke's
The Notebooks of Malte Laurids Brigge

*T*he self may be divided conceptually in numerous ways, for it is a composite of diverse elements and forces, competing and complementary, and that scheme which adequately explains the position of the "I" and its status in relation to mind and body is awarded primacy. We may speak, as William James does, of a fourfold classification of selves into the material, the social, the spiritual, and the "pure," thus dividing and isolating the facets of human beings in the interest of identification. Similarly we can distinguish the empirical from the rational self as Kant does, just as he differentiates metaphysically between the phenomenal and noumenal egos, calling the latter real. Whatever arrangement or structure is proposed as explanatory, whether multiple or unitary in nature, it must not only measure up to philosophic canons of precision, scope, and coherence on the objective plain but also subjectively satisfy our self-awareness.

For we know ourselves introspectively with a vividness and immediacy that assures authenticity and constitutes the ultimate standard which all speculative theories of selfhood

131

must satisfy. The inner self of others is known by inference, extension, and empathy, by analogy and an intuitive process of recognition, but we are conscious of our own person in a deeper sense. Theories of the self, therefore, must be compatible and consistent with an internal sense of our individual being. In other areas, introspection is not necessarily authoritative but here it is the highest proof. The self becomes both subject and object; we are self-aware.

I know the "I" consists at least of that which wills my movements, electing to stay or escape; stand and be counted; make the best of things; choose the more rugged path; slip into retirement; love my neighbor; bar the door; sink or swim; seek satisfaction in saintliness, the pleasures of my body, the fulfillment of friendship, a growing bank account, the etherealized earth at sunset. I deliberate on what is best for me or you; imagine myths, utopias, and extravagant fictions; perceive the light from fireplaces or stars; dream of what the future holds and carry remembrances of what it held in the spectral past. I am that which loves and despises, feels jealous or indifferent, finds magic in the moment or is bored to the point of tears. In short, I am an entity that experiences, plans, evaluates, wills, anticipates, recalls, and otherwise interacts with the physical world. Although the "I" is not an object whose mode of existence enables it to be perceived by others, not an object like a rock or bear or tulip, my self is known principally by descending within myself. I am aware of a continuity inside providing a point of reference for past occurrences, present actions, and those events imagined in the future. There is an organization and integration recognizable to consciousness which rejects the notion that the self is an illusion, and resists the oceanic feeling as a seduction into madness.

More than our culture makes us reject the quandary of the philosophical Taoist Chuang-tzu, expounder and propagandist of the *Tao Te Ching*: "Once upon a time, I Chuang-tzu, dreamt I was a butterfly, fluttering hither and thither, to all intents and purposes a butterfly . . . suddenly, I was awakened. . . . Now I do not know whether I was then a man dreaming I was a butterfly, or whether I am now a butterfly dreaming I am a man." Unlike Chuang-tzu we do not confound the dream and waking worlds so radically, but possess a surer sense of both internal and external reality. At moments we seem to be insubstantial shapes moving through fantasy episodes, but the separation between appearance and fact is never actually in doubt. Similarly, although we can empathize with Madame Ackermann's *cri de Coeur* in *Pensées d'un Solitaire*, we cannot declare it universal truth:

> When I reflect on the fact that I have made my appearance by accident upon a globe itself whirled through space as the sport of the catastrophes of the heavens, when I see myself surrounded by beings as ephemeral and incomprehensible as I am myself, and all excitedly pursuing pure chimeras, I experience a strange feeling of being in a dream. It seems to me as if I have loved and suffered, and that ere long I shall die, in a dream. My last word will be, "I have been dreaming."

This same grasp of personal reality, undistorted by morbidity or indoctrination, enables us to remain skeptical toward any mystical identification of subject and object, or an alleged understanding of the self as an illusion held within the embrace of the all. The mystical union, in which sensations are melted and merged, one's bones become liquefied, and absolute unity is experienced with the world soul, appeals to our fear of separateness, our lonely individuality. We sometimes long for absorption into the vast dark of unconsciousness the way we want the oblivion of sleep, but, for good or ill, wishes do not necessarily correspond to realities. The universe exists independent of the heart's desires, not in conformity to our inner wants. However much our weariness, loneliness, or need for love may make us seek unity and oneness, our integrity will not permit self-deception. The reality of our individual selfhood is apprehended with an intensity that renders denial absurd; if the "I" is not real then everything is mere appearance without substance. Thus the Hindu equation of the individual and the universe, Atman and Braham as essentially One, violates our fundamental self-awareness as does Sufism, Neoplatonism, Christian mysticism, and Whitman's ecstatic spiritualism.

However, although we refuse to label the self as illusory and insist upon its individual reality, we do not regard it as primarily a physical entity. Both laypersons and philosophers customarily make a distinction between mind and body such that the former is identified more closely with the "I." A loss of self is not experienced, for example, when a limb is amputated, but selfhood is significantly diminished when our capacity to will, reason, or remember is impaired. Individuals who become senile and lose their capacity to think can more easily be regarded as changed people than those confined to a wheelchair. Someone handicapped by an awful accident may become embittered or saintly as a consequence of that condition, but if we then say he or she is a different person, that judgment refers to the internal change that resulted from the physical disability, not to the disability itself. In short, mind impresses us as being basic to the self; body is more peripheral and remote. It can even be regarded as inessential, in terms of which the notion of disembodied existence appears plausible and spiritual immortality becomes a logical possibility.

The primacy of the thinking mind so impressed René Descartes that it became the ground for his "indubitable" personal existence; he declared, ". . . my essence consists solely in the fact that I am a thinking thing."

Cogito ergo sum: I think, therefore I am. The body cannot be denied, but as the object of (fallible) sense perception it cannot be treated as central to the self either.

> And although . . . (certainly) . . . I possess a body with which I am very intimately conjoined I am only a thinking and unextended thing . . . this I, that is to say, my soul by which I am what I am, is entirely and absolutely distinct from my body . . . although my whole mind seems to be united to the whole body, yet if a foot, or an arm, or some other part, is separated from my body, I am aware that nothing has been taken away from my mind. (*Meditation* VI)

The distinction between mind and body is further defined by Descartes as follows:

> In the first place, then, I considered myself as having a face, hands, arms, and all that system of members composed of bones and flesh as seen in a corpse which I designated by the name of body. In addition to this I considered that I was nourished, that I walked, that I felt, and that I thought, and I referred all these actions to the soul. . . . I imagined (my soul) was something extremely rare and subtle like a wind, a flame, or an ether, which was spread throughout my grosser parts. . . . By the body I understand all that which can be defined by a certain figure: something which can be confined in a certain place, and which can fill a given space in such a way that every other body will be excluded from it; which can be perceived either by touch, or by sight, or by hearing, or by taste, or by smell: which can be moved in many ways not, in truth, by itself, but by something which is foreign to it, by which it is touched and from which it receives impressions. (*Meditation* II)

That is to say, there exists a category of activities and events such as experiencing ecstasy or anguish, deciding or ignoring, which are attributable to mind, and unlike physical occurrences they are neither localized on grids of time or space, nor capable of being observed by others. Nevertheless, it seems more adequate to associate the self with this realm than with that of corporeal reality. Although people can offer no proof of a public sort concerning, for example, their feeling of inner peace, and they are unable to trace this emotion to a definite point inside, or state its shape or color, they link their self more closely with this feeling than with a physical part such as a hand, which does have an observable form, size, texture, shade, hardness, and so forth. For this reason Descartes is not just making an autobiographical comment but is functioning as a spokesman when he declares himself a being "which doubts, which understands, conceives, affirms, denies, wills, rejects, and imagines."

However, by radically distinguishing mind from body, Descartes left as a legacy to philosophy the problem of how two such different entities could interact, and the reconciliation of the duality has plagued philosophers since the seventeenth century.[1] Obviously, human minds and bodies do influence one another, and if so, this phenomenon should be explicable. When we receive a physical wound the mental event of pain results; when we hear a sharp, loud noise we experience fear. Conversely, our thoughts direct us to speak and walk, will and desire; "the moving finger writes and having written then moves on" only as ordered by the mind. Common sense testifies to a mutual causation continually operative in our lives, but how the nonphysical interacts with the physical, and vice versa, is a matter for theoretical speculation. Other interactions, such as heredity × environment, are difficult to analyze but lack the mysteriousness present here.

One proposed explanation called *materialism* consists in the denial of mind as a spiritual entity and a reduction of activities traditionally attributed to mind as physiological processes. "Brain" replaces the term "mind"; or else a behavioristic explanation is employed to account for all phenomena. In either case, human beings are classed with other organic and inorganic objects, which are totally subject to physical laws, and can be operationally defined; the only difference is that of a higher complexity, hampering clear study. Since we have evolved through natural processes, a product and creation of brute nature, there is nothing unique about us, nothing that would warrant exemption from the type of explanations applied to other natural objects. Our neuromuscular activity as well as our gross behavior can be seen in other organisms not attributed with a spiritual center.

Furthermore, this theory not only claims that a physical explanation is appropriate and sufficient for all human activities but challenges the possibility of any evidence for mind. By its very nature mind belongs to an unknowable realm, a sphere to which no empirical evidence is relevant. It cannot be felt, tasted, or smelled; to touch or see it, or set up any criteria determining its presence is practically and theoretically impossible. Mind, by definition, transcends perceptual verification.

To ascribe events to mind as causal agent involves a similar verification problem. If my hand is burned when thrust into the fire, then a causal connection can be inferred; the sequence is repeatable, public, and observable. When I reach for my fork, a physiological sequence can be detected behind the operation: my muscles contracted on certain nerve impulses which in turn were triggered by certain neural events occurring in my brain. But what sort of evidence can be offered for the assumption that a nonphysical entity called mind caused the movement of my arm? Surely this is beyond all conceivable verification and thus permanently unknowable. On the strength of this last point it is sometimes further charged that the existence of mind can only be asserted using an argument from ignorance, as previously noted. We do not know what lies behind or beneath the physiological processes; consequently we claim that mind is this fundamental source. Obviously this is illogical, because the lack of knowledge cannot furnish grounds for a positive conclusion; a theory is neither proven by not having been disproven nor disproven by not having been proven. Such is the indictment leveled by "reductive materialism."

An opposite theory having some currency in philosophy maintains that body is explicable in terms of mind—a theory traditionally labeled *panpsychism*. On this reading the materialistic account is rejected because its empirical presuppositions are viewed as pure prejudices in favor of physical explanations. It is inconsistent with our experience of phenomena such as remembering, desiring, deliberating, and acting in terms of conscious purpose. To reduce phenomena of this sort to physiological proportions violates our deepest feelings that something other than a physical process is occurring when, for example, we are experiencing aesthetic joy or the emotion of love. It arbitrarily narrows human life by declaring that people cannot be anything other than that which is empirically verifiable. Such a reduction is not only repugnant and unnatural but depends upon an unfounded criterion for genuine knowledge.

As an alternative, consciousness can be awarded primacy and the reality of physical events occurring within an individual can become a matter of doubt. Viewed from within the context of mind, an allegedly physical event such as breaking a tooth is experienced as a sharp pain, a morning swim as a feeling of invigoration—a feeling brought about by a prior mental process of deliberation and decision. By analogy with our own minds, we could even attribute awareness in varying degrees to the entire range of objects in the world from stones to other people, for just as we know ourselves to lie behind that which is externally apparent, other objects, too, could possess spiritual centers of vitality within. In the case of plants and trees the level of awareness (and freedom) would be quite low; for fish and animals, somewhat higher. But analogically, a mode of consciousness could be asserted to reside within every object in the universe, and the aggregate of these spiritual centers may constitute reality.

Whether or not we feel persuaded to go this far, at least it seems plausible to credit our feeling of self-awareness and personal continuity, both of which resist being equated with an order of matter.

If we assert the reality of mind as well as body, we are faced with the theoretical problem of how interaction can occur, but at least we feel in harmony with our introspective knowledge of ourselves. In panpsychism and reductive materialism a certain consistency is gained at the expense of common sensibility and personal evidence, which concluded we are both mind and body, neither of which is reducible to the other.

If self, then, embraces mind and body, a further set of questions becomes relevant: To what extent are we physical beings and to what extent spiritual? The self cannot be identified with one's body since we are more than the sum of our corporeal parts, nevertheless, body seems to be a definite part of the self.[2] And although the self is closely associated with mind it is not just mind but something more encompassing.

If self were only that series of mental phenomena making up mind, then it becomes impossible to account for the fact of awareness; to quote J. S. Mill, we should have to "accept the paradox that something which *ex hypothesi* is but a series of feelings, can be aware of itself as a series," or that "I feel" is the same as "I know that I feel." Consciousness is not the same as self-consciousness.

What, then, are the boundaries of the self? How much or what portions of our bodies would have to be lost before we feel a diminution of selfhood? What is that thread of continuity running though various experiences which is the "I" possessing a history? When our physical being grows, decays, and changes through our lives, how is the self affected? How can the self reflect upon itself, be both subject and object; as William James asks, how can "I" contemplate "me"?

Related also are questions concerning the relation of the self to the not-self: What should necessarily be included as essential to the self and what should be excluded as antithetical to it? What lies outside as object of consciousness and what within as subject? The self may be held to include the persons one loves—one's mate, family, and friends—and one's property, especially things like tools worn from a lifetime of use, one's land and home, beloved books, a favorite armchair, or clothing that has conformed to one's body from repeated wearing as Thoreau describes in *Walden*: "Kings and queens who wear a suit but once, though made by some tailor or dressmaker to their majesties, cannot know the comfort of wearing a suit that fits. They are no better than wooden horses to hang the clean clothes on. Every day our garments become more assimilated to ourselves, receiving the impress of the wearer's character, until we hesitate to lay them aside, without such delay and medical appliances and some such solemnity even as our bodies." Sculptors like Rodin create unities that include several bodies comprising a new whole, or complete entities consisting of fragments of bodies such as torsos without arms. (See Rilke on Rodin.)

Or one can identify one's self with all humanity, enlarge the self to embrace the whole of humankind within one's consciousness as John Donne declares in his famous *Meditation XVII*: "No man is an island, entire of itself; every man is a piece of the continent, a part of the main; if a clod be washed away by the sea, Europe is the less, as well as if a promontory were; as well as if a manor of they friends or of thine own; any man's death diminishes me, because I am involved in mankind; and therefore never send to know for whom the bell tolls; it tolls for thee." Personal identity is at issue here as disclosed in reflective knowledge. How wide or narrow is the self? Is an individual, as James states, "the sum total of all that he *can* call his?" (*Principles of Psychology*).

We could also inquire as to what core or substance survives all changes and developments throughout one's personal life. Seemingly every facet of our being changes. Our thoughts, attitudes, aspirations, and values change from childhood to old age. Our memory may grow dim or be lost, our personality can vary from extreme compassion to bitter cynicism and misanthropy, our bodies undergo a virtual metamorphosis as every cell is replaced many times, and growth and degeneration proceed continually between birth and death. What, then, remains constant? The self will be whatever entitles us to declare we are the same person throughout, legitimately referred to by the same name. It is whatever constitutes the persistent pattern, the constant organization, that principle of personal unity underlying all change.

Such is the nature of the problem of the self, one of the key philosophic issues. But professional philosophers cannot claim exclusive rights in this area, and have not monopolized all discussion. Psychology has contributed insights and experimental evidence, and sociology has been concerned with the relationship between the individual and the family, institutions, society, and state. Most important for our purposes, a rich body of literature pivots round an exploration of personal identity and selfhood.

KAFKA'S *THE METAMORPHOSIS*

Franz Kafka's *The Metamorphosis* is an outstanding case in point, combining within itself an awareness of physical degeneration, culminating in death, and concern for identification of that inner essence that makes up the self.

At the beginning of the story we are presented with an incredible fact that contradicts our customary assumptions about the behavior of our bodies. A traveling salesman who goes to sleep as a man wakes up transformed into a beetle: "As Gregor Samsa awoke one morning from a troubled dream, he found himself changed in his bed to some monstrous kind of vermin." We immediately assume we have been plunged into a fantasy world and anticipate additional bizarre events, suspending disbelief and lending ourselves to the fiction. However, nothing further occurs of an extraordinary nature, and the sheer banality of subsequent events comes as somewhat of a surprise. In fact, the story proceeds with such a high degree of ordinariness and matter-of-factness that we soon cease to regard the initial event as impossible and treat the whole as acutely realistic.

At first, Gregor refuses to accept the truth of his transformation, dismissing his rigidity, convex back, and numerous waving legs as an illusion. He tries to return to sleep thinking that the absurdity will vanish upon reawakening but the impossibility of rolling over on his side forces him to accept his actual state (reality forcibly dispelling illusion). But he quickly adjusts to having a different form with relatively little resistance, and concentrates on coping with his daily routine in a new condition. He must catch the five o'clock train for his employer is intolerant of excuses and he is already overdue, so he tries to rise, put on his clothes, and pack his samples. But his body is awkward to maneuver, bulky, and inflexible. But puffing himself out he manages to slip the quilt to the floor, but getting up is more difficult. On his beetle back, lacking arms and hands, movement in any direction poses a problem, but by rocking back and forth Gregor finally swings his stiff form out of bed and onto the carpet. By this time the chief clerk at the office has arrived to inquire about his lateness, and he and Gregor's mother and father are pounding on the door. Attempting to gain time, Gregor tells them he is coming, and when they become insistent refuses to open the door to them. Finally, frightened of losing his job by the diatribe of the chief clerk, he heaves himself into a position from which he can unlock the door with his mouth. Kafka in his attention to realistic detail mentions that Gregor damages his jaws in turning the key in the locks so that brown fluid issues from his mouth, flows over the key, and drips onto the floor.

Throughout this time Gregor's only concern is with the immediate demands, with meeting the expectations of others. His condition generates some distress but he feels no genuine anxiety. He is upset at his sudden inability to control his movements but only because it hinders his customary response to the requirements of his employer and parents. In these first moments, which should have been filled with terror over the metamorphosis of his person, Gregor is intent only on the practical problems of managing his beetle body, and with explaining away his failure to perform his usual duties. Instead of being horrified he is apologetic and tries to placate the chief clerk. "But sir," he cries in a paroxysm of agitation,

> I'm just going to open the door this very minute. A slight illness, an attack of giddiness, has kept me from getting up. I'm still lying in bed. But I feel all right again. I'm getting out of bed now. Just give me a moment or two longer! I'm not quite so well as I thought. But I'm all right really. . . . Anyhow, I can still catch the eight o'clock train. I'm much

the better for my few hours' rest. Don't let me detain you here, sir; I'll be attending to business very soon, and do be good enough to tell the chief so and to make my excuses to him![3]

But Gregor's words are not understood by anyone but himself; the chief clerk hears only a nonhuman voice, uttering unintelligible sounds. And when the door is opened and he sees the beetle Gregor has become, he recoils with disgust. Gregor's shrill attempts at reassurance horrify him still more, and he bolts toward the staircase.

The reaction of Gregor's parents quickly changes from an initial grief over a son so radically altered to repulsion and fear. When, having fallen on his many legs, Gregor tries to overtake the chief clerk to persuade him against making an unfavorable report, his father drives him back into the bedroom with a walking stick and newspapers, stamping on the floor and hissing as though he were a loathsome creature. When Gregor becomes wedged in the doorway, his father pushes him forward so that he falls into the room bleeding freely, leaving "horrid blotches" on the white door, the oozing of his injuries.

Neither parent can retain a feeling of pity for their son in the face of such a monstrous change in his appearance, and, like Gregor, they soon become concerned with means of coping with the situation. In the days that follow, conferences are held about the family's financial state, wondering how they are to manage now that Gregor can no longer function as breadwinner. Previous investments cannot sustain them, so Gregor's father takes a position as a bank messenger even though he has not worked for five years; surprisingly enough, he thrives on the regime of activity.[4] Gregor's sister becomes a salesgirl, his mother does fine sewing at home, some jewelry is sold, lodgers are taken in, and the household help is reduced to one old charwoman who does heavy chores mornings and evenings.

Gregor is hidden away in his room out of sight because his appearance repulses everyone, and in his transformed state he is a social embarrassment. When the household cook leaves she swears a solemn oath not to say a single word to anyone about what had happened—"even without any prompting." Everyone is guilty of silent collusion in pretending that the household is well ordered or, at worst, that Gregor's condition is a temporary abnormality.

Only Gregor's sister, a young girl named Grete, shows compassion toward him, although her feelings probably have their origin in "childish thoughtlessness" as Kafka remarks, and an odd possessiveness is intermixed with her solicitude. Oddly enough, she is the one who ultimately reproves her parents for regarding the beetle as Gregor and says it must be gotten rid of. Nevertheless, she looks after Gregor at first, cleaning his room regularly and providing food suited to his taste twice a day: half-decayed vegetables; moldy cheese; thick, dried-out sauce, and the like. No one else can bear to enter the room, and even she is alarmed at the sight of him, so that out of consideration Gregor hides himself under the sofa whenever he hears her preparing to open the door. But eventually she tires of her role of caretaker and begins to carelessly push into his room with her foot any food that is available regardless of what Gregor had not touched of the previous meal. Streaks of dirt are left stretching along the walls, and wads of dust and filth accumulate in the corners unnoticed.

In response to this treatment Gregor, too, becomes indifferent, no longer bothering to turn on his back and scrape himself clean on the carpet every day but going about covered with dust, trailing hair and remnants of food after him. He degenerates in other respects as well, assimilating various insect characteristics until the metamorphosis is more nearly complete. His power to communicate using language, that *sine qua non* of humanness, disappears nearly at once, followed by a deterioration of his vision. "[D]ay by day things that were even a little way off were growing dimmer to his sight," Kafka tells us, "the hospital across the street, which he had used to execrate for being all too often before his eyes, was now quite beyond his range of vision, and if he had not known that he lived in Charlotte Street, a quiet street but still a city street, he might have believed that his window gave on a desert waste where gray sky and gray land blended indistinguishably into each other." The fact that his wounds heal so quickly leaving no trace of disability or discomfort makes him reflect "how more than a month ago he had cut one finger a little with a knife and had still suffered pain from the wound only the day before yesterday." Has his sensitivity diminished? he wonders, sucking greedily on some rancid cheese. And in time the considerateness upon which he prided himself gives way to a growing lack of concern about the effect of his appearance on others, an absence of shame.

From the outset he feels quite at home on his numerous thin legs; when underneath him, not waving wildly in the air, they are "completely obedient" and carry him in whatever direction he chooses. He takes to crawling over the walls, leaving a trail of sticky fluid from his soles, and especially comes to enjoy hanging suspended from the ceiling: "it was much better than lying on the floor; one could breathe more freely; one's body swung and rocked lightly in a state of blissful absorption."

This desire to crawl over flat surfaces at whatever angle also makes him want his room quite empty of obstructions, but when his sister, anticipating his wishes, attempts to remove the furniture, the vestiges of Gregor's identity and humanness revolt.

Did he really want his warm room, so comfortably fitted with old family furniture, to be turned into a naked den in which he would certainly be able to crawl unhampered in all directions but at the price of shedding simultaneously all recollection of his human background? . . . Nothing should be taken out of his room; everything must stay as it was; he could not dispense with the good influence of the furniture on his state of mind; and even if the furniture did hamper him in his senseless crawling round and round, that was no drawback but a great advantage.

Consequently, as his sister is moving his furniture, Gregor rushes out from under the sofa. Not knowing which one of his belongings to rescue first, and being struck with a picture on the wall of a lady in furs, he quickly crawls up to it and presses himself against the glass. The picture frame was something he himself had previously constructed, laboring over it several evenings after work. "This picture at least, which was entirely hidden beneath him, was going to be removed by nobody." If Grete tried to chase him down from the wall, he would rather fly in her face than give it up.

Gregor's mother, who has entered the room for the first time since the metamorphosis to help Grete remove the furniture, collapses at the sight of "the huge brown mass on the flowered wallpaper." Filled with self-reproach, Gregor runs into the next room to help his sister with medications, but Grete shuts him out and he is left in a state of despair "to crawl to and fro, over everything, walls, furniture, and ceiling," finally falling down onto the big table unconscious.

When Gregor's father returns he is told, "Mother has been fainting, but she's better now. Gregor's broken loose," which confirms his worst expectations that one day Gregor would do something awful. Filled with rage, he begins hurling apples at Gregor from a dish on the sideboard, one of which lands squarely on his beetle back and sinks in; it remains lodged there from then on, slowly decaying. The excruciating pain of the injury causes Gregor to lose consciousness again, and he would have died under the bombardment if his mother had not rushed forward and flung herself on his father's neck, begging for his life.

As a result of this incident, Gregor's powers of movement are permanently impaired but, strangely enough, his treatment improves. The apple sticking in his body serves as a reproach and a reminder that despite his repulsive form, he is still a member of the family and should be pitied, not abused. The door to the living room is left open for several hours in the evening so that he can silently watch the family at the lamp-lit table and overhear their conversation—which Gregor feels to be ample compensation for his worsened condition.

But the amnesty lasts only a short time; his care is soon neglected once again, and a second incident occurs which turns the family against him irrevocably. One night Gregor hears his sister playing the violin for the lodgers and, drawn almost irresistibly by the music, he crawls forward into the circle of listeners. "He felt as if the way was opening before him to the unknown nourishment he craved," Kafka explains. He also wants to indicate to Grete how much more he appreciated her playing than the lodgers who obviously were listening merely out of courtesy. But however sensitive Gregor's motives may be, his very presence is intolerable, and when the lodgers catch sight of him an ugly scene ensues. The upshot is that they give notice on the spot "because of the disgusting conditions prevailing in this household and family." The door closes; Gregor's father staggers to a chair, jerking uncontrollably; and his mother has a severe attack of asthma, coughing and gasping for breath. Grete alone keeps her presence of mind and takes charge.

With Gregor looking on she declares, "My dear parents, . . . things can't go on like this. Perhaps you don't realize that, but I do. I won't utter my brother's name in the presence of this creature, and so all I say is: we must try to get rid of it. We've tried to look after it and to put up with it as far as is humanly possible, and I don't think anyone would reproach us in the slightest. . . .

"He must go . . . that's the only solution, Father. You must try to get rid of the idea that this is Gregor. The fact that we've believed it for so long is the root of all our trouble. How can it be Gregor? If this were Gregor, he would have realized long ago that human beings can't live with such a creature, and he'd have gone away on his own accord."

In response, Gregor limps back to his room, and once inside the door finds that he is no longer able to stir his limbs. It comes as no surprise; rather it seems unnatural that his feeble legs had ever supported him. He sinks into a comatose state, thinking tenderly of his family and of the decision which he, too, shares that he must disappear. Shortly thereafter, he dies. The charwoman discovers the body in the morning and announces "It's lying there dead and done for!" to which Mr. Samsa replies, "Thanks be to God." The thing is gotten rid of behind the scenes and the family, in an excess of relief, board a tram for a day in the country.

What are we to make of this bizarre tale? Various interpretations seem possible and legitimate. On one reading, Gregor has metamorphosed externally into the insect which internally he had already become. Through a magical transformation his outward appearance has been brought into conformity with the quality of life he had been leading; his self is now a harmonious whole. Formerly, he had misled people into taking him for a human being, duping them like a conjurer or illusionist with a façade of humanness. Not by design but by reason of convention, people had concentrated their attention upon his visible form instead of the more essential constituents of selfhood lying within. Now the pretence has been exposed. No mistakes can be made in the face of such manifest truth. Rather than the metamorphosis being fantastic, it presents undeniable reality, a brute fact which neither Gregor nor his family can evade. It is rather Gregor's former state that was the lie, the deception in which everyone collaborated to keep a repulsive truth hidden away. Gregor's condition forcibly brings to consciousness that which previously had been consigned to subconscious depths: the realization that he had been living the life of an insect throughout. Honesty of this magnitude is too painful to be borne; evidence so concrete must be secreted out of sight and all reminders obliterated.

The fact that Gregor does not seem genuinely astounded at the change, that he readily accepts the sudden degeneration to an insect form and concerns himself with practicalities involved, suggests that the change was not viewed as radical. Except for various adjustments in his way of moving about, Gregor copes with his condition quite naturally. There is an almost immediate acceptance of the state of affairs, almost a feeling of relief at being done with the demands of being human and responsible. No claustrophobic writhings, no resistance against an intolerable mode of being characterize his response. It is as though he half expected this occurrence, that it is part of a natural evolution, not at all foreign to his nature.

Gregor's family, too, seem to accept his beetle form without regarding the overnight change as impossible. After the initial shock they are more upset than unbelieving. They feel sorrow, some degree of outrage and hopelessness, at times as if "they had been singled out for misfortune" despite the fact that they had "fulfilled to the uttermost all that the world demand of poor people." And Grete spares her parents anguish by keeping the insect behind locked doors. But no one rejects the possibility that Gregor could occupy the body of an insect.

What could be more fitting, more uniquely just, than for a man like Gregor to become a beetle? He had lived a daily, nonthinking existence, making his rounds as a salesman in strict accordance with his employer's demands. Deviation from the routine never entered his mind. With his family economically dependent upon him, he met the requirements of a food-gatherer, foraging where he had to each day in dreary, repetitive labor. Apart from this role he does not seem to have done very much at all, which is exactly the point. Humanness and personal identity begin where activities directed at securing the necessities of life leave off. It is precisely with regard to human and individual qualities that Gregor is deficient. He had not developed himself in any significant respect but responded to practical needs, thus becoming more of a "thing" than a human being. To a creature like this, metamorphosis into an insect is perfectly appropriate: it is poetic justice.

According to another interpretation, Kafka is portraying the relationship of the self to one's internal and external being—examining in pure laboratory conditions, divorced from ordinary circumstances, the phenomenon of selfhood.

Within, Gregor is nearly identical with his former self; some degeneration occurs with respect to memory and feeling, but his character does not alter significantly. He is still the rather pitiful, timid creature.

Throughout all of his misfortunes, Gregor remains his amiable, other-directed self. When he can no longer be useful, he tries at least to be inconspicuous, to keep out of the way so that the family routine is not disrupted. And when the regard of others no longer justifies his existence, he obediently removes himself by dying; to offend or trouble other people by his presence would be unthinkable and out of character. Gregor is consistently self-effacing to the point of extinction.

Outside, however, the change is entire. The metamorphosis is, in fact, primarily external in nature, a corporeal phenomenon with some internal ramifications. Nevertheless, in a real sense this physical change is a life-determining one: it circumscribes Gregor's actions. Although he does not award the metamorphosis much importance, the new shape prescribes the limits of his freedom, determining how he can behave in the world. The shell that he inhabits makes ordinary movement impossible: he cannot lie on his back in bed, or walk upright; he cannot bend at the waist or curl into a ball to sleep. Without hands he is deprived of extension and dexterity and must use his mouth to accomplish rudimentary tasks. Without the protection of bones he is prone to serious injury, so that a thrown apple becomes a lethal weapon.

Even if Gregor remains largely unaffected inside by the change in his physical being, the reader feels a sense of claustrophobia, empathizing with a man trapped in an insect body. And through this experience one comes to realize the physical limitations surrounding any person—that we are all forced to endure life within a body which determines us yet seems peripheral to our selves. Gregor's beetle shape as an extreme merely dramatizes the disparity we experience between our personal aspirations and the necessities and restraints imposed by the body. Our spiritual reach always exceeds our physical grasp.

There is something outrageous in the fact that we are enclosed within our skin, inseparably joined to a physical self, "chained to a dying animal," and subject to all vicissitudes of the flesh. The truth of our corporeity wounds our pride by making the material world our master. It pricks the bubble of autonomy and assaults the assumption that our lives are meaningful. That we need to eat regularly, to feed the body we inhabit, adds insult to injury; that we must eliminate wastes is humiliating; that approximately one-third of our lives must be spent sleeping is beyond endurance. Everywhere we turn our bodily requirements assert themselves and demand satisfaction upon pain of death. Our richest moments of creativity must yield to the necessity for rest; our highest aspirations are stymied or defeated by fatigue, illness, and old age. This side of the grave, we cannot disassociate ourselves from our bodies either physically or metaphysically, yet we cannot achieve complete integration either. In a sense, our physical part always remains foreign to us, sometimes a nuisance, sometimes a pleasure, but never fully identified with the "I." As Sartre says, "nothing" really separates us, and this abyss of nothingness is unbridgeable.

Perhaps, then, Kafka is depicting this bifurcation through a radical physical transformation that underscores the separation between body and self. Perhaps he is saying: "We are not our bodies and yet we are, for a sudden metamorphosis to an insect form would affect our existence."

A third interpretation treats the story as a metaphor standing for the inevitability of degeneration and death. We all undergo a metamorphosis of growth and decay from our first to our last moments of life, and although the change occurs gradually and not overnight, the same process operates upon us. Toward the end, our skin, too, is crusty and easily cracked, our voices are heard by others as shrill and piping, our eyesight becomes poor, and our sensitivity decreases. We must be careful in our movements because our bodies do not respond as they once did and, being brittle, are vulnerable to the slightest injury. Getting out of bed in the morning becomes a laborious procedure, for we have grown stiff in the night, and when we get up our legs have grown so thin that they hardly support us. Foods which formerly appealed to our taste are no longer tempting, and we become finicky about our diets, eating far less and then only things that do not require strong teeth. When we speak no one understands us or pays attention to our words; we cannot communicate with others even though our thoughts make sense to ourselves. A nuisance to everyone because of the care we require, repulsive to the sight in our decrepitude, we feel apologetic for our existence and stay out of the way. Finally, surrounded by neglect and rejection, we slip into death to everyone's relief.

All of these manifestations of aging are familiar, occurring in all human beings during their life cycle, but the metamorphosis is painful and for that reason it is concealed and repressed. Out of a deep-seated psychological need we engage in an elaborate pretense that people remain the same. Like Gregor's family we collaborate in the lie that nothing changes, that everything continues on unaltered, people, work, life itself. We counter the reality of mutability with a myth of sameness and admit no contrary evidence. To acknowledge the reality of change would foster intolerable anguish, for change tokens the approach of death and the awareness of death must be repressed above all. Therefore, we employ devices such as repetition and routine, the habitual performance of regular chores, and ritualize our activities for the sake of proving that life is durable. Society functions toward the same end through the forms of ceremony and tradition, silently delegated to institutionalize the illusion. Order must be maintained, the structures of civilization must be perpetuated in defiance of the flux of nature outside the city gates. Human existence must be made to appear stable and constant, not a great booming, buzzing, blooming confusion! Man must identify with the eternal, the ideal, the timeless, the abiding, otherwise the fragility of being in the world is exposed and the fearful prospect of annihilation floods into consciousness.

The Samsa family is representative in this respect, neither psychotic nor honest about the fact of change. They are normal middle-class people typically bourgeois in their outlook. Prague is their home but they could be resident anywhere, for they are a universal and not a national type. Consequently, they have maintained the illusion of immutability, and react with hate and horror toward Gregor's transformation as the blatant contradiction of their pretense. For a son to become an insect implies the transiency of all states, no matter how securely reinforced by social conventions. The beetle represents impermanence, and the hatred of it, as excruciating truth, is only partially allayed by the remembrance that it is a son and a brother, just as the treatment of repellent old people is only somewhat softened by the memory of what they were formerly.

The dominant need, then, when confronted with a threat of this dimension is to preserve the false world in which one can live free from the anxiety of change and the final, unavoidable metamorphosis. Thanks are offered to God when the insect is removed from sight and mind; order can be restored, death excluded from daily consciousness, and an artificially slowed and sweetened life resumed. And the apple that Gregor's father hurls at him is a protest against a son who has betrayed the family's world. By his radical change, Gregor has made the nightmare visible, and a patriarchal act is appropriate to chase away the monstrous and reinstate the pleasant, to reject the catastrophic and recover the sense that life is uniform and changeless.

We cannot blame Gregor's father for his reaction because we share his anxiety. Without even having the beetle's presence visibly before us, by just reading the tale we feel strangely disturbed as though Kafka had penetrated our defenses and touched a basic source of anxiety. Not only do we keep at bay the reality of change by living a routine existence, but we act as though the customary sequences of events were the only possible ones. We assume that nature is uniform so that the unexpected could not occur, hoping to create the reality by believing in it. We predict and plan our lives on the assumption that the future will duplicate the past even though it never has, and we bring to the world clear expectations regarding the behavior of objects and events. Even though the unanticipated is always occurring, we label it unusual, and call disasters freak happenings despite the daily newspaper reports; we need consistency.

Regardless of these attempts to stabilize our existence, we carry within us an unacknowledged realization of the precariousness of life. Kafka reminds us that one day everything could be different; we might wake up changed and the people surrounding us might behave in new ways. One day the continuity of our lives just might be shattered, for there is no compelling reason why not, and discontinuities such as having an embolism rupture or being paralyzed by a stroke are actually a part of the order of nature.

Sleep is a particularly frightening phenomenon in this regard, for we are never quite sure of the character of our resurrection in the morning. In sleep we dwell in a dark and mysterious place, a realm of unconsciousness to which we have yielded ourselves, and when we return it is as travelers from far away; like Proust, we can "hear the echo of great spaces traversed," we can "measure the resistance." And when we come to the surface there is some uncertainty about our own identity, and a feeling of relief when we see our belongings just where we left them. Of course, we do not really expect our furniture to move during the night, but at the same time it is reassuring to see the dresser and chest of drawers still in the same place.

To a certain extent we feel that the behavior of things about us depends upon our perception of them and, when we are not watching, they could change position or shape in extraordinary ways. That is why we breathe more easily after we awaken and see that everything is as it was, including ourselves.

Gregor's metamorphosis would occur as he "awoke one morning from a troubled dream." If one's customary expectations were to be transformed into the fantastic, it would be at this moment when one has the weakest hold on normal experience. With only the slight forewarning of a troubled dream, Gregor finds his form has suddenly changed entirely; henceforth he must operate according to different laws altogether. Internally his identity has largely been retained, but outside the dreaded change has occurred, and being long dreaded it offers no shock.

From that point on Gregor's self includes an insect body with which he must perform his daily tasks and by which he is known to others. In this degenerated condition he must live out his last days, deformed and crippled, an object of horror and detestation to all who see him, for they are viewing their own future. Barred from his employment, he cannot even obtain respect as a provider. He is totally deprived of status in the family or the world outside and must remain in his room dehumanized and without dignity. Under these circumstances he gladly relinquishes his hold upon life and welcomes death no less gratefully than those about him.

Each of these interpretations provides insight and perspective into the story without doing violence to the content or departing from the basic text. Consequently, we may ascribe validity to each of them as well as crediting various other theories concerning Kafka's meaning that are less closely connected with the problem of the self. For example, an easy identification is possible between the author and his insect-man, Kafka and Samsa, and not only with regard to the similarity of name (which may offer a clue). According to a heavily Freudian interpretation, Kafka is portraying himself as a gigantic insect that plagues his hardworking, innocent family. He is here confessing his feeling of inferiority before his father, a particularly awesome, patriarchal figure, who always conveyed the impression that his son was a disappointment to him. Or perhaps Kafka is expressing his own repressed parricide desires in reverse by showing his father on the verge of infanticide. (Reversal is, in fact, a device that Kafka frequently employs, knowingly or unwittingly, and one found in dreams and myths—the censored product of the unconscious mind.) An Oedipus situation would then have been depicted of a highly autobiographical kind.

However, the philosophical interpretation seems more persuasive than the psychological—which is not to say that they are mutually exclusive; it is a matter of weight and emphasis. Whatever else Kafka may be saying, he is clearly concerned with the relationship between one's internal conscious life and the bodily form in which one is encased.

RILKE'S *THE NOTEBOOKS OF MALTE LAURIDS BRIGGE*

The German poet Rainer Marie Rilke has a similar preoccupation with self and reaches almost the same conclusions regarding identity. To Rilke the self lies within, and one's bodily parts belong more to the world than to oneself. He treats the essential self as coextensive with the dynamic, vital forces operating within. These upsurging forces unify and contain one's physical parts, which are no more than incidental appendages.

In Rilke's partly autobiographical prose work *The Notebooks of Malte Laurids Brigge*, this distinction is illustrated particularly in passages relating to hands and faces. For example, Malte describes how, as a child, he had hunted with his hand in dim light beneath a table for a red crayon he had dropped, until he could no longer retain a feeling of ownership toward the hand or assume responsibility for its conduct:

> . . . the darkness was growing more penetrable. I could already distinguish the wall at the back, which ended in a light-colored molding . . . above all I recognized my own outspread hand moving down there all alone, a little like an aquatic animal, examining the ground. I watched it, as I remember still, almost with curiosity; it seemed as if it knew things I had never taught it, groping down there so independently, with movements I had never noticed in it before. I followed it up as it pressed forward. I was interested in it, ready for all sorts of things. But how should I have been prepared to see suddenly come to meet it out of the wall another hand—a larger, extraordinarily thin hand, such as I had never seen before. It came groping in similar fashion from the other side, and the two outspread hands moved blindly toward one another. My curiosity was not yet used up, but suddenly it came to an end, and there was only terror. I felt that one of the hands belonged to me, and that it was committing itself to something irreparable. With all the authority I had over it, I checked it and drew it back flat and slowly, without taking my eyes off the other, which went on groping. I realized that it would not leave off; I cannot tell how I got up again. I sat deep in the armchair, my teeth chattered, and I had so little blood in my face that it seemed to me there could be no more blue in my eyes.[5]

In this experience Malte's hand has grown disassociated from him to such an extent that it has almost become part of the world of things, outside the boundaries of the self. His hand is on the verge of joining in the play of shadows and animals, of gaining its liberty, free from allegiance to the head. It moved "down there" in unfamiliar depth "like an aquatic animal, examining the ground"; it knew things, independent of Malte's skills, and groped in the semidarkness "so independently" with movements "never noticed in it before." Malte watches it "almost with curiosity"; he follows it up as it presses forward "ready for all sorts of things" (or "ready for anything to happen" according to Linton's translation). The hand has become separate and autonomous so that Malte cannot predict what it will do next; he observes it as an object of interest having little relation to himself. Gradually, curiosity gives way to the fear that it might elect to remain apart from him and stay to live among objects with which it shares a greater affinity.

Faces, too, are more a part of matter than an expression of ourselves; they mirror the world or present a response to it, an interpretation of it, a pose for it. Some poets assume that after a certain age a person is responsible for his face—that it reflects one's character, happiness, or sufferings—but Rilke regards faces as having been determined by external forces. To Rilke they bear an impress from without rather than being molded from within. In this they are closely identifiable with hands that are scarred and lined from outside contact. Witness the following passage:

> But the woman . . . she had completely collapsed in herself, forward into her hands. It was at the corner of rue Notre-Dame-de-Champs. I began to walk softly as soon as I saw her. When poor people are reflecting they should not be disturbed. Perhaps their idea will yet occur to them.
>
> The street was too empty; its emptiness was bored; it caught my step from under my feet and clattered about with it hither and yon, as with a wooden clog. The woman startled and pulled away too quickly out of herself, too violently, so that her face remained in her two hands. I could see it lying in them, its hollow form. It cost me indescribable effort to stay with those hands and not to look at what

had torn itself out of them. I shuddered to see a face from the inside, but still I was much more afraid of the naked, flayed head without a face.

The woman's face has more in common with her hands than any other body part and consequently remains attached to them when she looked up, leaving the raw flesh of her head revealed. If it remained exposed long enough, it would harden into a new face with features formed by the pressures of the world like "the tender exposed inside of a fruit which spoils upon contact with the air."

To Rilke, faces and hands belong to the physical universe substantially removed from the inner self; we are alienated from both. Furthermore, hands undergo a separate development, having their own culture and history, their own moods and preferences. Faces, too, have an independent and varied life. Some people wear one face consistently while others change their faces regularly during their lifetime:

To think . . . that I have never been aware before how many faces there are. There are quantities of human beings, but there are many more faces, for each person has several. There are people who wear the same face for years; naturally it wears out, it gets dirty, it splits at the folds, it stretches, like gloves one has worn on a journey. These are thrifty, simple people; they do not change their face, they never even have it cleaned. It is good enough, they say, and who can prove to them the contrary? The question of course arises, since they have several faces, what do they do with the others? They store them up. Their children will wear them. But sometimes, too, it happens that their dogs go out with them on. And why not? A face is a face.

Other people put their faces on, one after the other, with uncanny rapidity and wear them out. At first it seems to them they are provided for always; but they scarcely reach forty—and they have come to the last. This naturally has something tragic. They are not accustomed to taking care of faces, their last is worn through in a week, has holes, and in many places is as thin as paper; and then little by little the under layer, the no-face, comes through, and they go about with that.

In one of Rilke's early poems he describes the face of a dying poet that seems to be returning to nature. It had long been part of nature, but at last it is to be reunited with its source. "Few people realized how much his face was already a part of the meadows, the waters, and the distances," Rilke remarks; "the landscape was still trying to reach him even at the moment of death."

Elsewhere Rilke declares that faces are never sufficiently plastic to reflect our inner personalities, therefore, to be devoid of a face is best of all; the *Nichtgesicht*, or not-face is ideal. "Has the forest a face?" Rilke challenges.

Does not the mountain basalt stand faceless there? Does the sea not raise itself without face, up from the ocean floor; is not the sky reflected within, without forehead, without mouth, without chin?

Do not animals come to us sometimes as if they were pleading: take my face. Their face is too heavy for them and because of it they hold their tiny little soul too far into life . . .

Rilke pleads for the absence of a face not just because it is alien, but because it constitutes a threat to the self. Faces are disguises that tend to assimilate and determine the wearer; we tend to respond to the role suggested by our appearance and to act accordingly. Through our faces the world penetrates us and stamps its features upon our souls.

Rather than being a means of projecting our personalities, the face enables the world to invade our self, using the medium of suggestibility. Operating on misguided assumptions, we look in the mirror to discover our identity and carry away that concept of ourselves reflected in the glass. But by this process we allow the world to displace our self. Faces are a mode of self-estrangement, not an organic secretion of ourselves, crystallized and representative. Mischief begins when we fail to treat the face as a mask and become the comic or tragic character of the mask; then a threat to our personal identity is engendered.

The analogy with clothing is unmistakable and, in fact, Rilke treats them as fundamentally the same. Unlike Thoreau, Rilke feels that dress is as external as faces, and both threaten the wearer. In *Malte*, he describes a childhood experience in which he made a game of dressing up in various old clothing found in an attic trunk until the game turned deadly and terrifying:

> It was then that I first learned to know the influence that can emanate directly from a particular costume itself. Hardly had I donned one of these suits, when I had to admit that it got me in its power; that it prescribed my movements, my facial expression, yes, even my ideas. My hand, over which the lace cuff fell and fell again, was anything but my usual hand; it moved like a person acting; I might even say that it was watching itself, exaggerated though that sounds. These disguises never, indeed, went so far as to make me feel a stranger to myself; on the contrary, the more varied my transformations, the more convinced did I become of myself. . . . I did not notice the temptation in this rapidly growing security.

One day Malte uncovers a virtual treasure chest of clothing for a masquerade: women's dresses, Pierrot costumes, braided Turkish trousers, Persian fezzes, wraps, shawls, veils, and masks. Mesmerized, he tries on numerous articles of clothing at once, creating a grandiose effect. But in parading before the mirror he overturns a table, shattering several porcelain and glass objects. This frightens him and he attempts to remove the costume to repair the damage, but the inevitable happens: the costume will not come off. "I pulled at all my garments, but they clung only the tighter. The cords of the mantle strangled me, and the stuff on my head pressed as though more and more were being added to it."

Malte rushes to the mirror to undo the fastenings, but this only exacerbates the situation:

> for this the mirror had just been waiting . . . it imposed on me an image, no, a reality, a strange, unbelievable and monstrous reality, with which, against my will, I became permeated: for now the mirror was the stronger, and I was the mirror. I stared at this great, terrifying unknown before me, and it seemed to me appalling to be alone with him. But at the very moment I thought this, the worst befell: I lost all sense, I simply ceased to exist. For one second I had an indescribable, painful and futile longing for myself, then there was only he: there was nothing but he.

The costume has taken over the wearer, imposing its own identity and dispossessing the person within—which is the great danger of role-playing. We may impersonate the person suggested by our appearance so convincingly that reversion to our true self becomes impossible. We have become the costume and no longer possess a personality distinct from the impersonation. The attraction of role-playing is that we feel protected by the layer of pretense, and we fortify ourselves with façade upon façade until we feel completely secure, but at the same time we are imprisoning ourselves and eroding our identity. Soon we are nothing but layers without a core, like an onion; our self has been displaced.

Rilke's own unusual upbringing in which he was raised as a girl until the age of five, had dresses, had long hair, and played with dolls, undoubtedly influenced his concern with costume, but his insights transcend mere autobiography.[6] The problem of protecting the self against the identity imposed by masks, roles, and costumes is universal in nature.

In Rilke's vision the self lies underneath both clothing and skin, metaphysically beneath bodily parts all of which contain the world's meanings and not our individual significance. The "I" can be understood only through "interior apprehension," which discloses upsurging, spontaneous forces as the quiddity of each person's being. Beyond this, Rilke interprets the universe in terms of basic life urges and a pervasive will-to-be suggestive of Schopenhauer and Nietzsche. For example, he does not see a cathedral as a static architectural object, an accomplished fact, but sees molten rock heaping itself up until it petrifies in the air and the surrounding houses are shocked speechless by the volcanic eruption. He sees statues as sunning themselves in gardens, and single flowers standing up and shouting "red" with frightened voices. Trees stand still "as though they could not find their way in the mist," and when a windowpane falls clattering, "its big splinters laugh, its little ones snicker." Lengths of fine lace are gorgeous plants unfolding their gigantic leaves with tendrils that grope for one another as though they were dizzy. And houses arranged round a square pile on top of one another, wanting to see everything.

The vital element in objects or people is not the extant and frozen surface, which is only manifestation, but an underlying spirit continually materializing itself. As a part of the physical universe human beings share in this process; our essence, too, lies within and what's more, can be understood as indwelling. It is this knowledge that Rilke would have us realize—that the selfhood of any person is unconnected with his empirical part; it is privately understood. Through his writings Rilke invites each of us to share his conviction that spiritual centers, resident deep within the body, create and sustain our fundamental selves.

Perhaps he is right. Some poetry is also truth.

NOTES

1. Descartes was not the first to present the problem, in fact, a mind/body dualism is implicit in everyday language that reflects ancient and natural thinking, but he is responsible for making the issue an important concern of modern philosophy. Descartes's conjecture was that the pineal gland accounted for the interaction—a theory usually ranked as a philosophic curiosity along with the "double aspect" theory of Spinoza and the "parallelism" of Leibnitz.

2. It is one thing to distinguish between mind and body, quite another to say that mind can exist even when body has ceased to exist—as doctrines of spiritual immortality claim. There is no logical inference from dualism to disembodied existence. A separate argument is required to establish life after bodily death.

3. Willa and Edwin Muir's translation will be used throughout.

4. When Gregor emerges from his room for the first time after the metamorphosis, he is astonished at the change his father has undergone: ". . . could that be his father? The man who used to lie wearily sunk in bed whenever Gregor set out on a business journey; who welcomed him back of an evening lying in a long chair in a dressing gown; who could not really rise to his feet, but only lifted his arms in greeting, and on the rare occasions when he did go out with his family . . . walked between Gregor and his mother . . . muffled in his old great coat, shuffling laboriously forward with the help of his crooked-handled stick. . . .

"Now he was standing there in fine shape, dressed in a smart blue uniform with gold buttons, such as bank messengers wear; his strong double chin bulged over the stiff high color of his jacket; from under his busy eyebrows his black eyes darted fresh and penetrating glances; his one time tangled white hair had been combed flat on either side of a shining and carefully exact parting."

Both father and son seem to have undergone a metamorphosis, but of opposite kinds, varying inversely in relation to each other.

5. R. M. Rilke, *The Notebooks of Malte Laurids Brigge*, trans. M. D. Herter Norton (New York: W. W. Norton, 1964). All references will be to this edition unless otherwise specified.

6. Through Malte's reflections Rilke describes the hermaphrodite status he held as a child: "[T]here was a time when Maman wished I had been a little girl, and not this boy that once and for all I was. I had somehow guessed this, and I had hit upon the notion of sometimes knocking in the afternoon at Maman's door. Then when she asked who was there, I took delight in answering from outside, 'Sophie,' making my voice so dainty that it tickled my throat. And when I entered then (in the little, girlish housedress I wore anyway, with sleeves rolled all the way up), I was simply Sophie, Maman's little Sophie, busy about household duties, whose hair Maman had to braid." Kafka suffered because he was not manly enough for his father; Rilke disappointed his mother by not having been born a girl.

SELECTED BIBLIOGRAPHY

*T*he selected bibliography below is intended as a guide for independent investigation of philosophic concepts in literature. The novels and plays listed range from works of outstanding quality to genuinely great literature, and are grouped according to the four philosophic topics discussed in the main body of the book. The emphasis is more on "classical" than contemporary literature, and includes works from all over the world.

All of the works have been chosen for their strong philosophical content. Although each contains several concepts, they're grouped according to the philosophic idea which predominates. The perceptive reader will no doubt want to alter the list, to add or subtract some books or, perhaps, reassign others to different categories (e.g., *Sapho* and *Camille* might be placed under the same heading). This seems not only legitimate but a necessary concomitant of the type of perspective which the author wants to foster.

1. Libertarian and Deterministic Perspectives

Aeschylus	*Agamemnon, The Persians, Prometheus Bound, Seven Against Thebes*
Balzac, H.	*Eugenie Grandet*
Butler, S.	*The Way of All Flesh*
Cervantes, M.	*Don Quixote*
Corneille, P.	*Horace*
Dreiser, T.	*An American Tragedy*
Euripedes	*Alcestis, Bacchae, Iphigenia, Medea*
Hardy, T.	*The Dynasts*
Homer	*The Iliad, The Odyssey*
Hugo, V.	*Les Miserables*
Ibsen, H.	*Doll's House, Ghosts*
Mann, T.	*Buddenbrooks*
Pushkin, A.	*The Captain's Daughter*
Racine, J.	*Phaedra*
Shakespeare, W.	*Henry VI, Richard III, Romeo and Juliet*
Sholokhov, N.	*The Silent Don*
Sophocles	*Oedipus Rex*
Warren, R. P.	*All the King's Men*
Webster, J.	*The Duchess of Malfi*
Zola, E.	*Nana*

2. The Good and The Right

Alcott, L. M.	*Little Women*
Balzac, H.	*La Recherche de l'Absolu*
Bunyan, J.	*Pilgrim's Progress*
Cather, W.	*A Lost Lady*
Clemens, S. L.	*The Adventures of Huckleberry Finn*
Cooper, J. F.	*The Leatherstocking Tales*
Crane, S.	*The Red Badge of Courage*

Dickens, C.	*David Copperfield, Oliver Twist, Pickwick Papers, A Tale of Two Cities*
Dos Passos, J.	*U.S.A.*
Dostoevsky, F.	*Crime and Punishment*
Duerenmatt, F.	*The Visit*
Dumas, A., fils	*Camille*
Eliot, G.	*Romola, Silas Marner*
Flaubert, G.	*Madame Bovary*
Gogal, N. V.	*Dead Souls*
Hawthorne, N.	*The Scarlet Letter*
Lope de Vega	*Fuente Ovejuna*
Moliere	*Le Misanthrope*
Pushkin, A.	*Eugene Onegin*
Rabelais, F.	*Gargantua and Pantagruel*
Scott, W.	*The Heart of Midlothian, Kennilworth*
Shakespeare, W.	*Macbeth*
Shaw, G. B.	*Man and Superman*
Silone, I.	*Bread and Wine, The Secret of Luca*
Sophocles	*Oedipus at Colonus*
Stowe, H. B.	*Uncle Tom's Cabin*
Swift, J.	*Gulliver's Travels*
Thackeray, W.	*Vanity Fair*
Wallace, L.	*Ben Hur*

3. THE PROBLEM OF EVIL

Bernanos, G.	*Joy*
Dante	*The Divine Comedy*
Dostoevsky, F.	*The Brothers Karamazov*
Hamsun, K.	*Growth of the Soil*
Hugo, V.	*The Hunchback of Notre Dame*
MacLeish, A.	*J.B.*
Mann, T.	*Doctor Faustus*

Manzoni, A.	*The Betrothed*
Marlowe, C.	*The Tragical History of Dr. Faustus*
Shakespeare, W.	*King Lear*
Strindberg, A.	*The Father, The Spook Sonata*
Tolstoy, L.	*The Death of Ivan Ilyitch*

4. *SELF: THE MIND-BODY PROBLEM*

Balzac, H.	*Le Père Gorlot*
Boccaccio	*The Decameron* (esp. Fiammetta's tale of Tancred and the Golden Cup)
Camus, A.	*The Stranger, The Plague*
Chekhov, A.	*The Seagull*
Clemens, S. L.	*The Prince and the Pauper*
Conrad, J.	*Lord Jim, Victory*
Daudet, A.	*Sapho*
Defoe, D.	*Robinson Crusoe*
De Maupassant, G.	*Une Vie*
Du Maurier, G.	*Trilby*
Eliot, G.	*Adam Bede*
Fitzgerald, F. S.	*The Great Gatsby*
Goethe, J. W.	*Wilhelm Meister*
Hudson, W. H.	*Green Mansions*
Huxley, A.	*Brave New World*
Ibsen, H.	*Hedda Gabler, Peer Gynt*
James, H.	*Portrait of a Lady*
Joyce, J.	*Portrait of the Artist as a Young Man*
Kafka, F.	*The Castle, The Trial*
Kipling, R.	*The Light That Failed*
Lagerlof, S.	*Story of Gosta Berling*
Lawrence, D. H.	*Sons and Lovers*
Meredith, G.	*The Egoist*
Miller, A.	*Death of a Salesman*

O'Neill, E.	*The Hairy Ape*
Orwell, G.	*1984*
Sartre, J.-P.	*Nausea*
Shakespeare, W.	*Hamlet*
Stendhal	*The Red and the Black*
Stevenson, R. L.	*Dr. Jekyll and Mr. Hyde*
Thoreau, H. D.	*Walden*
Wilde, O.	*The Picture of Dorian Gray*

INDEX